Developing Topic Work
in the Primary School

Developing Topic Work in the Primary School

Edited by
C. Sarah Tann

The Falmer Press
(A member of the Taylor & Francis Group)
London • New York • Philadelphia

UK   The Falmer Press, Falmer House, Barcombe, Lewes, East Sussex, BN8 5DL

USA   The Falmer Press, Taylor & Francis Inc., 242 Cherry Street, Philadelphia, PA 19106-1906

First published 1988 Reprinted 1989

Library of Congress Cataloging in Publication Data is available on request

ISBN 1 85000 300 9
ISBN 1 85000 301 7 (pbk.)

Jacket design by Teresa Dearlove

Typeset in 11/13 Bembo by
Mathematical Composition Setters Ltd, Ivy Street, Salisbury

Printed in Great Britain by Taylor & Francis (Printers) Ltd, Basingstoke

Contents

Contents

Acknowledgements

Many people have helped to contribute to this book through helpful comments and discussion during the preparation stages. I would like to thank, in particular, Professor John Chapman of the Open University, and Mairi McLeod and the first cohort of students on course 6203 at Oxford Polytechnic.

Finally, I would like to thank the publishers, Cassell, for permission to use Figs. 2.1, 2.2, 2.3 from Pollard, A. and Tann, S. (1987) *Reflective Teaching in the Primary School*.

Part 1:
A Framework for Topic Work

Introduction

Good topic work is the epitome of all that is best in British primary schools. It is an all-embracing way of working and one which is infinitely flexible. It therefore requires tremendous skill and sensitivity on the part of the teacher. This is particularly demanding in terms of monitoring what the children are learning and of managing the opportunities for learning so as to maximize the benefit for each child.

The purpose of this book is to support those who want to develop the potential of topic work. This can best be done by sharing the experiences of teachers who have been excited by the learning which they have witnessed taking place through topic work. The book is written at a time of intense educational upheaval: a time of review and reform concerning what our schools should be teaching and how they should be monitored. The subject-based curriculum framework and objective testing would seem to be at odds with the topic work way of learning. Therefore, those of us who believe in the value of topic work need to be very clear as to our reasons for doing it, much more rigorous in our understanding of it and especially in our monitoring of the children's achievements.

A period of such intense activity is a particularly important time for teachers to re-examine the teaching and learning which occurs in their own classrooms. Teachers must be able and willing to clearly articulate the reasons for their policies and practices to their professional colleagues (teachers and advisors), their partners (children, parents, governors and local communities) as well as their political masters (local and national).

It is essential for teachers to be able to share their understandings about what to teach, how to teach, why and with what results. In the present clammer for 'basics' it becomes increasingly important for teachers to be able not only to defend but also to develop the 'other' areas of the curriculum and other ways of teaching and learning.

As a contribution to the re-examination of our practices, part 1 of this book outlines a theoretical framework for topic work in the primary curriculum. Chapter 1 focuses on why we do topic work and on its role and status in the curriculum. Chapter 2 focuses on the range of current practices and analyzes what children learn by doing topic work, particularly with regard to information skills and 'learning to learn' through integrated, investigatory work which they undertake.

Chapter 1:
The Rationale for Topic Work

Sarah Tann

What is Topic Work?

It's always different and it's always exciting.

We think of lots of questions. Then we choose which ones to start with. Then we think how to find the answers. There's lots of thinking in topic work.

It's what our teacher tells us about the Tudors on Tuesday and Friday afternoons.

We work in groups and we find things out. Then we do a display.

We choose something then we look things up and write things down.

Each person has to find out all they can about something and write it in their folder. I'm doing birds.

You do lots of different things all about something that interests you. You have to include a report, an experiment or a survey or something with numbers, then you do some art work and a poem. It takes about a month. Then you do another one.

These children clearly experience 'topic work' in very different forms.

Yet their differing perceptions identify a number of common variables which have become an integral part of topic work, even though the same variable can be put into practice in diverse ways. These variables include:

Control: teacher initiated/individual choice;
Content: specific 'subject' area/integrated 'theme'/or individual 'interest';
Context: individual/group/class;
Purpose: accumulating new knowledge/process of finding out;
Process: looking up and writing down/investigating;
Product: individual folders/joint display ...

From an observer's viewpoint, despite the variations, 'topic work' has become a standard feature of the primary classroom. HMI (DES, 1978) found that 49 per cent of schools spent between 10–25 per cent of timetabled hours on topic and 5 per cent spent more than 25 per cent of their time on topic.

However, these 'percentages' cover many different kinds of work which are labelled in many different ways. Terms such as topic, project, thematic work all refer to related activities. The terms themselves are often confused, not to mention confusing, for each of these terms have been used in a variety of ways by writers. The terms have also been interpreted differently in different local authorities, by individual schools and by the teachers involved.

Despite such differences, there are common threads which link such terms together and at the same time distinguish them as the 'other' part of the curriculum in contrast to the 'basics' — the 3Rs (Alexander, 1984). This crude practical distinction of 'other' and 'basic' is, however, false and misleading. It assumes that topic work is either 'higher' than basic and in some way more difficult, or, that it is more peripheral than the basics. Topic work, in fact, provides a meaningful and purposeful context in which the 'basics' are essential as tools for finding out and communicating the results of the investigations undertaken in topic work.

For the purposes of this book, topic work will be defined loosely to include an approach to learning which draws upon children's concerns and which actively involves them in the planning, executing, presenting and evaluating of a negotiated learning experience. In this form of topic work 'control' is a shared responsibility. Because of this, topic work encompasses an infinite variety in terms of 'content', 'contexts', 'purposes', 'processes' and 'presentations'. Topic work cannot be defined in any fixed curriculum or organization terms: it is more a way of learning and a way of teaching.

Why Do We Do It?

A topic work approach to learning has a long pedigree. For example, in the eighteenth century, Johnathan Swift spoke of himself as a speculative investigator, a 'projector'. This concept is very much in tune with the process-orientated, exploratory approach, which encourages active involvement by learners in defining and discovering their own knowledge.

Many of Dewey's writings, in the early years of this century, indicated a strong emphasis on the importance of starting from the child and the significance of first-hand experience in education. His discussion of a heuristic model of learning and teaching has much in common with Swift's notion of being a speculative investigator and with later writer's identification of the stages and types of 'topic' work.

In England, during the inter-war period, what came to be known as the Dalton Plan was one of the first widely recognized attempts to allow children to work on their own and to take greater control of their own learning. During this same period, the notions of curriculum as being activity-based and of the importance of the autonomy of the learner was enshrined in the first of many official reports on education (Board of Education 1931).

These notions of activity-based, investigative, autonomous learning were incorporated and legitimated by the Plowden report (CACE, 1967). Their logical extension into cross-curricula activity in a range of learning contexts introduced new criteria for curricula content and organizational contexts as well as creating new demands for monitoring the teaching-learning environment. For example:
on content

Rigid division of the curriculum into subjects tends to interrupt children's train of thought and of interest and to hinder them from realizing the common elements of problem solving (para 535).

The topic cuts across the boundaries of subjects and is treated as its nature requires (para 540).

Integration is not only a question of allowing time for interests which do not fit under subject headings; it is as much a matter of seeing the different dimensions of subject work and of using the forms of observation and communication which are most suitable to a given sequence of learning (para 542).

on context

One topic for the time being can involve both group and class interest, and may splinter off into all kinds of individual work (para 541).

on process

At its best the method leads to the use of books of reference, to individual work and to active participation in learning (para 540).

Children are not assimilating inert ideas but are wholly involved in thinking, feeling and doing. The slow and the bright share a common experience and each takes from it what he can at his own level (para 542).

Initial curiosity ... leads to questions and to a consideration of what questions it is sensible to ask and how to find the answers... Essential elements are enquiry, exploration, and first-hand experience which may mean expeditions (para 669).

The DES (1975) adds to this:

There is a sequence of ways in which children gather information:
finding out from observation and first-hand experience;
finding out from someone who will explain and discuss;
finding out by listening;
finding out by reading. (12.7)

Furthermore, just as different tasks call upon different reading skills so they also demand a variety of modes of recording. Note making and other forms of record keeping associated with pupils can be valuable ways not simply of learning, but of learning to learn (12.8).

Finally, Plowden (CACE, 1967) outlines school policy issues for topic work:

> There is little place for the type of scheme which sets down exactly what ground should be covered and what skill should be acquired by each class in the school. Yet to put nothing in its place may be to leave some teachers prisoners of tradition and to make difficulties for newcomers to a staff who are left to pick up, little by little, the ethos of the school. The best solution seems to be to provide brief schemes for the school as a whole: outlines of aims in various areas of the curriculum, the sequence of development which can be expected in children and the methods through which the work can be soundly based and progress accelerated. It is also useful to have a record of experiences, topics, books, poems and music which have been found to succeed with children of different ages. (para 539).

Other characteristics claimed for topic work might include:

(i) advantages which can be gained in terms of:
    (a) responsiveness to children's needs and interests in particular;
    (b) opportunities for the development of the whole child — social, emotional, physical, aesthetic, and cognitive;
(ii) approaches to learning which allow:
    (a) sharing of the responsibility for planning the work;
    (b) flexibility in the way in which 'knowledge' is classified;
    (c) variety in the organization of how the learning is done;
(iii) active involvement by the participants through:
    (a) purposeful, speculative approaches to the issue being investigated;
    (b) practical, investigatory procedures;
    (c) productive, problem-solving aspects to the outcomes;
    (d) reflective, evaluatory attitudes to the whole enterprise.

What is the Role of Topic Work in the Primary Curriculum?

The Relationship of Topic Work to Curriculum Organization

A further aspect in considering the role of topic work in the primary school curriculum is to identify the different types of topic work. This could then be related both to alternative ways of organizing the curriculum and also to different ways in which children learn. Such an analysis could help us to clarify the potential that topic work could play in children's learning.

Three main alternative types of topic work are distinguishable in terms of their relationship to curriculum organization:

(a) *Concept-based*: This might take the form of a study of 'change and continuity' in our town. A series of activities may be planned which could easily be identified with associated humanities subjects such as history and geography. A number of different skills could also be developed, including observation and drawing of buildings, mapping the town and doing a survey of current amenities. This kind of approach is sometimes identified as social, environmental or local studies.

(b) *Interest-based*: This might start from a class visit to a place of interest, or from some event that arouses interest in the children. For example, a child's remark about 'milk growing in bottles' may spark off an interest in dairying and food in general. A series of activities may develop which can be identified with a wide range of subject areas, or forms of knowledge, which are all loosely linked by the theme of food, for example, where milk comes from, which foods are good for us and why, how to grow runner beans, from which countries our foods come, the cultural and religious significance of certain foods, and also some cooking activities including weighing, timing and pricing.

Interest-based topics could just as easily be sparked off from fictional or aesthetic sources as it could from a factual one. A particular story, a piece of music, a song or a picture could form the basis of children's investigations.

(c) *Problem-based*: This kind of work is often very specific and intended for a shorter period of time. A child may ask, or be set a task to make a lighthouse with a flashing light. This would involve exploring with batteries and bulbs, then designing and constructing a working model.

Although approaches are sometimes combined, these distinctions do highlight two aspects of curriculum integration through topic work and, therefore, the breakdown of subject boundaries suggested by Plowden: how closely 'subjects' are intermeshed and how many 'subjects' are intermingled. The greater the integration, the greater portion of the day is usually devoted to integrated topic work. Thus, a fully integrated curriculum may result in children spending the whole day following topics of interest, through which knowledge, concepts, skills and attitudes can be developed in a meaningful context.

The Relationship of Topic Work to Children's Learning

Even though a topic may integrate different 'subjects', tasks are usually tackled in some kind of order. This possible sequencing of tasks within the topic raises two different sets of issues which have implications in terms of where 'control' for topic work should lie and whether control over the ordering of content is important. First, it would be necessary to consider whether tasks need to be sequenced in a particular order. If so, the second issue is to decide on which criteria tasks should be sequenced.

The choices depend on our view of knowledge and our view of how children learn. For example, if a curriculum is viewed as a means of imparting specific knowledge (selected because of its worth, interest, or relevance), then it is likely to be sequenced with reference to propositions about the logical structure of that knowledge and in terms of its conceptual basis. If, however, the curriculum is viewed as the accumulative experiences of the children interacting with their environment and with each other, then its sequence is less likely to be determined by logical strictures than by the anticipated psychological patterns of children's learning. This will be less likely to fit a neat linear model of learning, where certain forms of learning are seen as a step-by-step progression (Gagne, 1975), but may be better represented by a spiral model, where children meet a concept or skill and then encounter it again when they may develop their understanding of it further (Bruner, 1977).

Other learning theorists suggest that children learn in 'leaps' which may involve a sideways move where the child may consolidate or apply some new understanding, or where the child may skip certain steps/ concepts which might be logically related and return to them when it appeared psychologically relevant to the child. Alternatively, Piaget and his workers have provided considerable evidence for the developmental stages of children's development in thinking — from activity-based 'motor' and 'concrete' stages to abstract 'formal operations'. Subsequent researchers have since greatly modified the original ages at which such stages might be expected, suggesting that children can think in much more sophisticated fashion, if actively engaged, at much younger ages than was first imagined (Donaldson, 1978). Clearly such differences have implications when considering the variables of control and progression within topic work.

Further issues concerning the way children learn also need to be considered. This involves attention to 'learning style' in both its cognitive and its personality aspects. Learning style refers to the dominant approach to learning that an individual naturally tends to use. Particular learning strategies and attitudes are already established by the age of 6, although in later years individuals usually learn to adopt a range of approaches which gives that learner greater flexibility. Whilst there is no single 'best' style, certain styles have been found to be more useful in particular circumstances. Hence the ability to modify our style to suit a task is one indication of a mature learner.

Many dimensions have been identified as key components of 'learning style'. For example:

wholist/serialist (Kagan and Kogan, 1970; Pask, 1976): from wholists who like to grasp the broad outline and fill in the details later (at the risk of superficiality), to serialists who prefer to build up the picture piece by piece (at the risk of failing to see the relationships between the pieces and the overall significances);

field-dependent/field-independent (Witkin *et al*, 1977): from field-dependents who like to use general context and own external experience to interpret or solve a problem (at the risk of being trapped by their previous experience), to field-independents who prefer to solve a problem by analyzing and manipulating the problem's internal components (at the risk of reinventing the wheel);

divergent/convergent (Torrance, 1962): from divergers who rely on inspirational flair and imagination (sometimes erratic), to convergers who look for the 'right' answer and prefer closed situations (sometimes blinkered);

impulsivity/reflexivity (Kagan *et al*, 1964): from impulsives who storm a task, to reflexives who prefer to chew things over, sometimes endlessly.

extroversion/introversion (Eysenek and Cookson, 1969): from extroverts who are outgoing but sometimes over-dependent on group stimulus or security, to introverts who are more 'private' but sometimes unable to collaborate with others.

Apart from such learning styles, there are other variables we need to consider, such as the medium for learning and the motivation for learning. For example children respond very differently if the learning is enactive, iconic or symbolic — where it might require motor/tactile, visual/graphic, or numerical/literary skills (either listening/talking or reading/writing). Further, motivation in different forms affect learners differently — whether intrinsic, collective, extrinsic or coercive.

All these factors need to be considered when analyzing the learning opportunities in topic work so that the children's learning experiences can more easily be appreciated.

What is the Status of Topic Work in the Curriculum Debate?

The Evidence Concerning Topic Work

The curriculum changes that are currently being discussed have partly been in response to periodic criticism of the way in which the primary curriculum in general, and topic work in particular, have been thought to operate in practice.

One of the first such criticisms which hit the headlines was contained in what came to be known as the Black Papers (1969a and 1969b). This was reported as a sweeping condemnation of what was thought to be the 'wild progressives' that were taking over the classrooms. The so-called Plowden revolution (for which the ORACLE research at the end of the seventies found scant evidence) was accused of throwing out structure and discipline with a subsequent lowering of standards. The 'child-centred' approach was described as merely indulging children's whims, resulting in a 'ragbag curriculum' which was a 'magpie collection of bits and pieces' because teachers were 'abdicating' their responsibilities.

Nevertheless, there were grounds for serious reflection. The sixties had witnessed a number of changes. These were firstly of an organizational nature — at a school level where the 11 + selective exam began to be phased out, and at a classroom level where teachers were having to cope with 'mixed-ability' classes and to find alternative forms of grouping the children and teaching them. With the inclusion of children of different ability levels, tensions were experienced with the traditional subject-segregated knowledge-orientated curriculum and with existing teaching techniques. Initiatives were needed to try to overcome both these issues. Many of these met with difficulties for a number of reasons, not least the need for adequate support for staff to help them to meet the new demands. Attempts to integrate areas of the curriculum, through topic work for example, was one way of trying to provide opportunities for greater flexibility so as to meet different children's needs and interests.

However, both Bullock (DES, 1975) and HMI (DES, 1978) found evidence of negative aspects associated with the way topic work operated in practice. For example, there was often too much copying and frequently an unrigorous approach to learning. Bullock noted that children were unable to summarize or to read selectively. Similar findings were reported by Lunzer and Gardner (1979) who also found that children lacked a sense of purpose and relied on their perceptions of what the teacher wanted to guide their efforts. Lawson (1979) reported that:

> An examination of topic work done in many schools reveals it to be bland and vacuous. The traditional notion of a body of knowledge to be transmitted by the teacher had been replaced by a view which sees a learning of 'the processes' as all important... It doesn't matter what project or topic you do as long as it satisfies three basic criteria. Firstly it has to stem from the child's interest or, at least, be seen to be 'relevant'. Secondly it has to be done in as non-directed a way as possible and thirdly it should not be subject to critical assessment outside reference to the child's estimated academic potential.

Clearly, there were many instances where the high ideals for topic work have been misinterpreted and misapplied. An all too accurate account of this devastating triviality of what sometimes goes by the name of 'topic work' is neatly explained by the character of Victor in Jan Mark's novel *Thunder and Lightnings*. Victor has done 'fish' three times. He draws pictures of fish (which all look remarkably alike) with a bit of writing every four pages. He does fish because it's easy and he doesn't care about them. He doesn't do anything he's interested in because if he had to do it, for the teacher, instead of wanting to do it, for himself, it would kill his interest.

This type of 'topic work' deserves to be criticized.

Subsequent research (Southgate, 1981; Avann, 1983) identified the fact that teachers themselves frequently lacked the skills necessary for topic work — in particular 'information skills'. Others found them hard to label and still harder to teach. Neville and Pugh (1975 and 1977) revealed that few 9-year-olds who knew how to read also knew how to use books for information and that few had received any instruction. Sayer (1979) found similar results with 11–14-year-olds. A further finding from Neville (1977) showed that little measurable progress was noted after a year of teaching. She concluded that the teaching of information skills needed consistent and prolonged support backed by a well-articulated, whole-school policy.

More recent research has begun to identify possible ways to help teachers give more support to children in topic work. Wray (1985) suggests that a paramount requisite is for teachers to decide what precisely their purposes are; to determine a systematic way of achieving these in a gradual, sequential and cumulative fashion; and to develop a system of record-keeping. Some general principles in trying to establish such a policy might be to avoid a separate skills approach (DES, 1975), to avoid leaving such skills to develop 'naturally' (Winkworth, 1977), to give practical guidance in a 'real' context (Lunzer and Gardner, 1979), and to openly discuss and make explicit the strategies which the children use thus developing a 'meta-language' to support the necessary 'meta-cognition' (Selmes, 1986; Nisbet and Shuksmith, 1986).

The Framework for Analyzing the Primary Curriculum

The renewed concern with the curriculum was one of the reasons which led Sir Keith Joseph, then Secretary of State for Education, to initiate a further examination of what schools were and should be teaching. In response to this HMI first produced a series of reports about what was happening in primary schools, secondary schools, first and, finally, middle schools (DES, 1978, 1979, 1982, 1985). This was followed by a series of discussion documents covering most aspects of the curriculum. The first of these, 'Curriculum 5–16' outlined a possible framework for discussing the contents of the curriculum.

HMI suggested seven 'areas of experience' which realigned the usual 'subject' divisions. The new groupings were:

aesthetic and creative	mathematical
human and social	scientific
linguistic and literary	technological
moral	physical
spiritual	

This would seem to be favouring compartmentalism rather than integration of the curriculum. HMI refers rather briefly to topic work as having 'potential advantages in facilitating sustained work on themes which children find interesting and relevant... Yet it can be difficult to ensure that there is sufficient progression and continuity particularly for older children' (para 16). HMI suggests that there may, on the other hand, be limitations in a curriculum which is no more than 'a list of subjects.' Clearly, they are reluctant to support either view, or to suggest how the advantages of both could be balanced.

An alternative way of integrating the curriculum is offered through the notion of 'elements of learning': knowledge, concepts, skills and attitudes which cut across subject divisions. HMI suggests that the criteria for selecting content (knowledge and concepts) should be that it is 'worth knowing, capable of sustaining pupils' interest and useful to them at their particular stage of development and in the future' (para 92). Skills — variously defined as the 'capacity or competence' to perform a task (how well), or, use of the 'techniques' necessary to perform a task (how to) — were claimed to be important in that they are applicable in a variety of contexts and therefore give pupils confidence and satisfaction from achieving useful goals at appropriate levels of achievement. Skills, the document continues, are best acquired in the course of activities that are seen as worthwhile in themselves (para 99). Key skills were listed as:

communication	physical and practical
observation	creative and imaginative
study	numerical
problem-solving	personal and social

Suggested attitudes included:

honesty	initiative
reliability	self-discipline
tolerance	

These sets of skills and attitudes are problematic in themselves. They could perhaps be useful as a starting point for teachers and children to explore, as a first step towards identifying the aspects of learning that occur during topic work or which could be conceived of as objectives for topic work.

However, the very notion of a 'core curriculum' causes considerable concern from many quarters. Among the issues that it raises are:

(i)   Does the notion of a 'core curriculum' undermine the child-centred philosophy of primary education?

(ii)   Will the existence of a 'core curriculum' undermine the professional autonomy of individual teachers and schools?

(iii) Will it alter the status of the generalist primary teacher in favour of 'subject specialists'?

(iv)   How can a single 'core curriculum' hope to meet the infinitely varied needs of children in different areas of the country and the particular needs of children who vary so considerably at the same age?

(v)   Who will decide the 'core curriculum' and how often will it be updated?

(vi)   How will it be resourced?

(vii) How will its success be measured?

However, the notion of a 'core curriculum' need not necessarily strike terror into the hearts of the supporters of topic work. A 'core curriculum' can take many forms. Richards (1982) reminds us of some important distinctions. The guidelines could exist at a number of different levels and with differing degrees of detail. He suggests three levels, ie national, local authority and school levels, and two degrees of detail, ie fine and coarse grain. It would seem unlikely that any part

15

of the United Kingdom would ever see a uniform, detailed set of specifications for every lesson for every year group in every subject. Nevertheless, it does seem likely that a 'coarse grained' national framework will be suggested, based on 'areas of experience' and 'elements of learning', and that this will be linked to detailed pupil profiles which will record children's achievements over the years. At the individual school level, schools will be encouraged to make explicit a fine grained framework for school curriculum policy which can serve as a reference point by which performance can be appraised.

Some reassurance for the supporters of topic work can be gleaned from the latest DES document, *The National Curriculum 5–16* (DES, 1987). The document stresses that 'legislation should leave full scope for professional judgment and for schools to organize how the curriculum is to be delivered in the way best suited to the ages, circumstances, needs and abilities of the children in each classroom' (para 27). Also, 'that there must be space to accommodate the enterprise of teachers ... sufficient flexibility in the choice of content ... to develop new approaches, and to develop those personal qualities which cannot be written into a programme of study or attainment target' (para 27). Furthermore, 'the description of the national curriculum in terms of foundation subjects is not a description of how the school day is to be organized and the curriculum delivered' (para 22). Hence one can assume that integrated, investigatory topic work will still be possible — so long as the (subject-based) objectives can be identified and monitored.

Nevertheless, the issues listed above concerning the 'core curriculum' have profound implications for the character of primary schools. The more curriculum issues are decided 'outside' the classroom — whether in the form of guidelines from the DES or by local governors in individual schools — the more the opportunities may be diminished for a 'topic work' way of teaching and learning. For, this approach presupposes that opportunities exist for the motivation and stimulus for a particular piece of investigative learning to come from children and their experiences. It also presupposes that the actual form of the investigation will be negotiated between the teacher and children. Hence, the 'curriculum' which emerges is based on responses to, with and from the children and teachers, not something which is predetermined and imposed on them.

The fears about professional autonomy and accountability are of continuing concern. Schools have, since 1980, been required by law to state their curriculum aims and to have such a statement available, in particular, to parents. This has mostly resulted in an extended version of the school brochure, which many schools already produced as basic information to give to families with children entering the school. Since then, changes in the composition and role of governing bodies have decreased the proportion of teaching members and increased the powers of the governing body to decide curriculum matters.

Paradoxically, it is often through topic work that parents are most actively involved in their child's learning. For, topic work draws from the child's experiences and children are encouraged to bring information and artifacts from home. Topic work also draws upon the locality, in terms of the human — often parent — and physical resources. The freedom to take advantage of such resources is an important asset that teachers can mobilize with their children.

In an era of accountability, such as the eighties are proving to be, we must expect that the teaching profession will not be excluded from the increasing demands of 'clients' to be allowed to know what is happening, why and how well. As a profession we need to be able to articulate the principles of our practices, communicate them to the children, parents and community and to justify the position of trust and confidence in which we are placed. However, it is also important to secure the conditions under which teachers can operate as professionals and be given the time, space, resources and opportunities to extend and act upon their professionalism.

Is There a Future for Topic Work?

If we return to the *Curriculum 5–16* document (DES, 1985b) we find that there were a number of key terms which were offered as a framework for discussions concerning the 'core curriculum': breadth and balance, relevance, differentiation, continuity and progression. Many of these are, in fact, also integral to the aims of topic work.

However, each of these terms raises particular issues and it is not yet clear how these terms are being interpreted by those responsible for drawing up a 'core curriculum'. For instance, breadth/balance is something to which many would subscribe in general, whilst interpreting 'balance' to emphasize different issues. It is possible to balance (give equal time/equal status) to different 'areas of experience', or, it is possible to try to find a 'balance' between specialism and generalism either within or across 'areas of experience'. Relevance is similarly open to a variety of interpretations. Curriculum content may be considered in terms of being 'relevant' to whom, for what, in the short or long-term, as perceived by whom?

The notion of differentiation is also ambiguous. Whilst many might try to differentiate tasks so that they match the ability levels of individual children (itself a very difficult task), should we also different-iate to match different 'needs' and 'interests'? How can these be identified? Should we take this to mean what is interesting TO the child, or what is IN the child's interest. How is this to be determined? HMI also suggest that there should be differentiation of teaching approaches (from practical to abstract) and of pacing (para 123). What about differentiation of learning contexts and locations?

It is, perhaps, the notion of continuity and progression which has become central in subsequent debates, for, as we have seen, it is precisely in this area that topic work has been most severely criticized. The notion of continuity and progression has been linked to the issues of monitoring children's ongoing work and also for recording achieve-ments (particularly for use at the points of transfer between different stages of the education system). Such monitoring is seen as inseparable from the teaching process, since its prime purpose is to improve learning performance, to match tasks to children's needs, to involve children in discussion and self-appraisal and to inform parents (para 134). Such monitoring also helps teachers to see how far their objectives are being met.

HMI recognize that monitoring takes place in a variety of ways: day-to-day observation of how pupils perform, by discussion and questioning, and through scrutiny of written work — all of which are an integral part of classroom activity (para 137). HMI go on to suggest that other, more objective forms of testing may also be used, however, 'they can too easily be divorced from classroom work and their use should therefore be limited' (para 139).

Continuity and progression could be achieved, HMI suggest, through a greater appreciation of what each school is doing (having explicit and available school curriculum policies), by using effective systems of records and 'by encouraging secondary schools to adopt the more exploratory styles of learning which are the characteristic of good primary school practice' (para 131).

Subsequent statements by the Secretary of State for Education, Kenneth Baker, made it clear that the government's concern was directed to finding ways of measuring 'achievements' by 'objective' and external tests, in an attempt to monitor 'standards' and 'audit' school effectiveness. Hence, it was suggested that 'benchmark' testing of children at 7, 11 and 16 years would be an essential 'objective' component of the drive to improve standards and to appraise the effectiveness of teachers as well as the progress of the learners. The costing and administrative procedures which would be involved have not yet been mentioned.

This use of tests was given greater prominence than any efforts to find ways of supporting the profession to develop ways of improving a range of monitoring techniques, including profiles. If standardized testing was imposed on the teaching profession it would be a very serious blow to the flexibility and self-directed investigatory way of teaching and learning which is epitomized by topic work.

Alternative informal yet rigorous monitoring techniques could, however, be used in a way that was integral to the ongoing work of the school and the learning experiences of the child, rather than outside those experiences.

One such suggestion, has been to develop and formalize the notion of 'contracts' between the teacher, parent and child. This could serve the multiple purposes of making expectations and goals explicit, communicating this to all parties concerned and at the same time focusing the learning so as to make it appropriate to the individual's needs.

This would need to be in association with a range of observational data concerning the processes of learning which the teacher could collect. This could be used by the teacher — with the child — in order to evaluate the child's learning. Such a system would, at the same time, provide a structured opportunity to develop skills in self-evaluation.

Hence, a key issue for the topic work approach to teaching and learning is how to combine two seemingly opposing goals: the 'romance' of the progressive ideology of the sixties which was rooted in child-centredness and individual response, with the 'rigour' demanded in the era of assessment, appraisal and accountability of the eighties where standardization through a core curriculum is offered as an instrument for progress. Because of the prominence given to this question of appraisal and assessment — whether by testing, monitoring, profiling, or contracting — it is an issue which will be explored in subsequent chapters, where a number of different approaches will be illustrated.

Chapter 2:
The Practice of Topic Work

Sarah Tann

What Is Current Practice?

Ask any set of teachers how and why they do topic work and you will probably get a different answer from each. Because topic work has become an expected feature of primary classroom life it has been fitted in to classrooms of very different types. These operate from a range of philosophical and pedagogical principles and include an additional variety of practices and believed policies.

A survey of forty teachers, mostly in three adjacent authorities in the Thames valley area, revealed widely differing practices on a range of criteria. These included:

control: to what extent the teacher or the children were the source of inspiration for the topic;

content: how narrowly or broadly the topic was extended and how deeply any aspects were investigated;

context: whether the topic was done as a class, a group, or individually, or, a mixture of each;

purpose/status: this was often indicated by the place that was ascribed for topic work and the time allowed;

processes: the degree to which the teaching/learning style was didactic- or discovery-oriented, and the nature and variety of resources used (primary/secondary);

presentation/audience: the range of audiences (teacher/peers/ parents), their role (assessing/appreciating), as well as the range of formats and outcomes;

records: whether any records were kept of the topics done, or of what individual children learnt.

Table 1 shows a number of hypothetical continuum derived from these responses from teachers. The variables which emerged are very much in common with those which could be identified in the children's perceptions, as illustrated at the beginning of chapter 1.

Table 1 is useful in a number of ways. First, it could be used so as to elicit what particular skills and attitudes (cognitive and social) might be developed by 'doing topic work' at each main point along each continuum. For example, in terms of control, if the teacher (without the children) makes the decisions about what to study and how, then the children will, in the first instance, learn to listen to the teacher and follow instructions. If the children make the decisions they will learn to listen to each other, offer suggestions, sort out and evaluate them, choose and then plan the follow-through. In terms of context, when children work in a school/class context, the learning includes a mixture of social and cognitive skills: children have the opportunity to learn from each other, to be interdependent, to plan together and make collective decisions and they will have a very real audience to whom to present their findings. Alternatively, if children work on their own the emphasis is on cognitive skills: skills of planning, executing and presenting their own work in their own way, as well as attitudes associated with autonomous learning, such as independence, responsibility and perseverance. A similar analysis can be made of the learning opportunities along each dimension.

Eliciting such skills could be used to form the framework of objectives for an individual teacher or school. Further, each set of skills may be considered important in themselves though some may be considered to be of greater value than others by different teachers. Some may be needed more than others by different children. Teachers, and children, could be encouraged to identify what they consider to be the relative 'value' of what might be learnt in each situation. This would reveal a ranking of objectives.

Secondly, the actual classroom practice of each teacher could be

Table 1: Characteristics of Integrated Curriculum Practice

(a) Control:	teacher-directed ←→	teacher and child(ren) negotiate ←→		child decides own project unaided or, children evolve group/class study.
(b) Content focus:	single/combined subject ←→	multidisciplinary ←→		main interest followed.
(c) Context:	whole class doing similar work ←→	groups doing related work ←→		individuals on own 'projects'
(d) Place in the curriculum:	'basics' in morning 'other' in afternoon ←→			fully integrated (throughout the day).
(e) Resources:	secondary sources (book-based) ←→	audio-visual, for example Watch programme (vicarious 'visits' and orally presented information) ←→		primary sources, first-hand experience (and experiments).
(f) Audience:	for teacher to assess ←→	for class to share ←→		for others to respond, for example, parents, community.
(g) Records:	none ←→	list of titles ←→	outlines of 'webs' kept centrally ←→	'log' kept by child, parent, teacher commenting on likes/dislikes evaluating hard/easy suggesting reinforcement/extension/new direction.

plotted along the continuum on each variable. In this way a pattern would be revealed which would indicate how any particular teacher was operating at that time. Having done that it would be possible to see to what extent actual teaching behaviour related to declared teaching objectives.

An examination of responses from the survey revealed that many teachers saw considerable potential for learning that was possible through topic work. They identified a long list of skills and attitudes related to organizational features of the classroom, independent of particular knowledge or concepts. However, they often lacked experience of alternative ways of 'doing' topic work in order to realize their own goals. It was very easy for teachers, and whole schools, to get locked in to doing topic work in a particular way which therefore limited the kinds of learning which could be expected.

This was especially true of schools which encouraged a highly individualized approach to topic, with each child choosing their own 'interest' and producing their own 'book' which was often very pleasing visually. Such children developed attitudes of perseverance and the skills of learning to work independently, of identifying a focus, of deciding what they wanted to find out where and how, they recorded relevant information and presented it clearly. There was often, however, little progression in their skill development, gaps in which skills they developed, and an *ad hoc* accumulation of knowledge without awareness of the underlying concepts. They also tended to miss opportunities to develop social skills through working together, to develop attitudes of respect and tolerance for each other's strengths and viewpoints, or to develop oral skills which can emerge through group discussion.

On the other hand there were schools which adopted a teacher-controlled approach and which focused carefully on conceptual progression through a predetermined set of topics for each year group, from which some choice was available. Often the whole class listened to the teacher as a key source of information, or followed a particular radio/TV programme. Individual folders were kept of the class experience. These children acquired a considerable amount of knowledge, but less in the way of 'learning to learn' skills.

However, there were instances where teachers deliberately encouraged different forms of topic work on different occasions in order to overcome the weaknesses of over-reliance on any one approach.

No school that was approached in this survey had a policy about topic work: two were beginning to tackle this. Another conspicuous aspect was that very few kept any form of records as to which topic any children had experienced. It is indeed easy to understand the fears about continuity and progression of the children's learning experiences in such situations.

Mismatch of Perceptions

A further survey of children's and teachers' perceptions of topic work showed wide discrepancies. For the children, topic work was knowledge orientated, 'to find things out', and resources were primarily book-based. For the teachers, topic work was process orientated, 'to learn how to learn', and resources were intended to be mixed and varied. The children perceived the context of topic work to be individual, but they would have liked to work in groups, whilst teachers regarded it as a group experience — though this appeared to mean seated IN groups rather than working collaboratively AS a group. Finally, the children saw topic work as looking things up in books and writing it down to put in their folder for the teacher to mark, whilst the teachers tended to view it as a general process of developing study skills.

These differences appeared to relate to differences between the intention (teachers' perceptions) and the actuality (children's perceptions). Somehow the teachers' purposes were not communicated to the children. The children did not see themselves as engaging in a long-term developmental activity but rather a series of one-off activities.

Recent evidence from the Schools Curriculum Development Committee (1985) has found an ambiguity in teachers' intentions which may help to throw light on these contradictions. The forty-three respondents reported their order of priority of topic work aims in the following way: first, relating to knowledge and concepts; secondly, skills; thirdly, attitudes; finally, classroom organization and management. However, when asked what were the advantages of topic work the order changed: top of the list was classroom organization and management; secondly pupil motivation; thirdly, the integrated curriculum; then, a low fourth, higher-order skills; finally, basic skills.

It would seem that the main reasons for doing topic work is that management is easier because the children are motivated (because they choose their own topics?) and extend their 'finding out' without regard to traditional 'subject' boundaries. This contributes to the impression that an integrated, child-centred approach is being implemented and the rhetoric of 'progressive' aims are being fulfilled (see also Leith, 1981).

It is easy to see what a travesty of the potential for learning can be experienced in such situations.

The children — and many of the teachers — responded to this form of topic work with mixed reactions. On the one hand most of those involved soon 'get the knack' of looking things up and writing things down and thus fulfilled the prevailing expectations and felt satisfaction. However, this soon become 'boring and samey'.

What was missing was any positive commitment from the children, any purposeful approach to finding out, any experimentation with alternative data sources, collecting techniques or presentation formats. There was little realization of what was being learnt (other than knowledge) because such aspects were often not articulated by the teachers or discussed. The dominance of the individualized approach restricted the opportunities for developing social skills, or of sharing and monitoring the processes and thereby providing an opportunity for developing evaluation skills and an understanding of what was being learnt. Finally, there was no real sense of audience which might well have provided a stimulus to set many of these other factors into motion.

How Can Teachers Respond to the Challenge of Topic Work?

Monitoring and Recording Topic Work

If we are to monitor the children's progress during topic work, it is also useful to analyze the progress of the topic itself. This could include a method of identifying the possible skills, attitudes, concepts and knowledge which might be developed.

One common practice in many primary schools is for teachers to spend part of their holiday planning next term's 'topic'. The plan is often drawn out in a 'topic web' which illustrates the associated ideas and activities to be developed. It then serves as a blueprint to guide the progression of work during the coming weeks. This plan tends to result in pre-packaged learning experiences and is usually based on the teacher's interpretation of such concepts as 'interests', 'relevance' and 'worth'. An elaboration of this is to map out an extended web, which distinguishes between the concepts, knowledge, skills and attitudes that might develop, or, to monitor the spread of activities across the curriculum in matrix form (Schools Council, 1983).

Alternative strategies are possible which give wider options. The teacher may plan a preliminary short topic just to 'get things going' at the beginning of term. Then, if some interest emerges from the children's activities and discussions, that interest can become the focal point for an individual child, group or whole class. The teacher,

Figure 1: Planning the curriculum: 'topic web' recording opportunities for developing concepts, knowledge, skills, attitudes. Age: 7-8 years. Focus: Teeth.

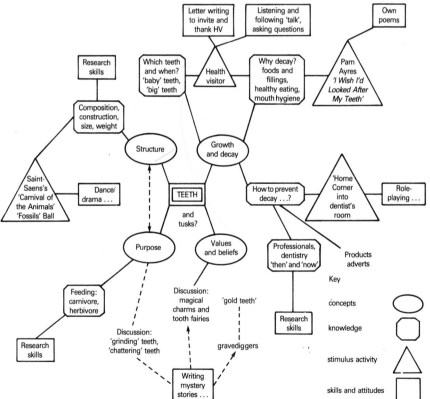

building on what the children have shown interest in, might anticipate alternative lines of development and identify what knowledge or skills would be developed. Only some of these might be taken up by the children. Other aspects may be added. This can be recorded in a 'flow chart' which can be updated throughout the life-time of the investigation. By this means a record is provided which shows the activities anticipated by the teacher and the children's actual activities. Although the teacher need not pre-package the activities, it is important to monitor and analyze the activities as they emerge.

A further way of monitoring the demands within a topic is by constructing a matrix. This can take many forms, for example one axis can list skills, attitudes, concepts and knowledge which it is anticipated

Figure 2: Monitoring the curriculum: flow chart recording growth of a class-directed project. Age 9-10 years. Focus: Food.

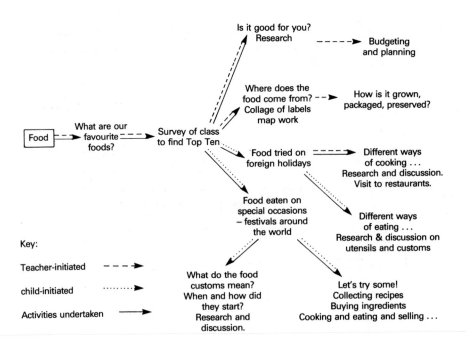

might be experienced and the other axis can list the different tasks or activities. The matrix can then be marked up by ticking which task provides an opportunity for which kinds of learning. By this time it is possible to monitor the distribution of task demands and identify the areas which, on this occasion, appear neglected. An alternative matrix could include 'areas of experience' along one axis and tasks along the other. Whichever format is used for monitoring the children's progress. This can be done by substituting the children's names for the tasks and then marking up the matrix to show how well each child met each demand. A graded system of shading is often used to show the different levels of achievement (see appendix).

Figure 3: Planning a curriculum forecast, on-going 'tabulated analysis' recording areas of experience over a series of activities. Age 5-6 years. Focus: Fairy stories.

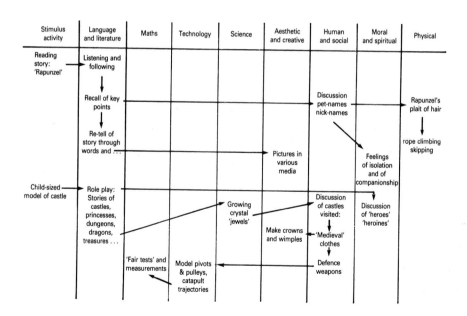

Sarah Tann

Monitoring and Recording the Children's Progress.

There are many ways in which teachers and children can help to monitor the learning in the classroom. Some of these are formative and integral to the dynamic teaching-learning processes. Some are summative and attempt to describe aspects of the stage of learning reached in terms of the product.

Observation

It is impossible for a teacher to be watching all of the children all of the time. Effective observation needs to be selective, either in who the teacher chooses to watch, what they watch for, when they watch and/or why.

Diary: the teacher decides who to watch in particular and why, then attempts to note down everything the child/ren does during the session/day/week depending on the reason for the observations. The diary notes then need to be analyzed so that an interpretation can be made and possible action taken.

Sign system: the teacher lists particular kinds of behaviour in which there is interest (for example, on/off task, asking/giving help, time-wasting) and marks up each time this behaviour is observed.

Systematic schedule: the teacher makes a comprehensive list of behaviours for observation, including categories of talk, and selects a particular period of time for observation (for example, ten minutes) and a specific time span (for example, fifteen or thirty seconds) for noting the precise behaviour occurring at that interval of time. This records the relative amounts of time spent on a variety of activities during the period of observation.

However, whilst such observation notes what the child/ren may be doing it does not reveal why.

Conferencing

This is a discussion between teacher and child, possibly in response to a set of observations, or as part of a review of work being done. The purpose is to encourage the child to explore their perceptions of what they are doing and how well they are doing it and for the teacher to help the child to understand their own learning achievements. Any misunderstandings about the purpose or standards of work can be discussed and future activities negotiated. By involving the child in their own learning and encouraging self-responsibility it is hoped that the child will be more motivated to learn. However, such extended discussions can pose management problems for the teacher until the class get used to the notion of 'conference time'. This could be a set period each day when the teacher can talk with a few individual children in turn.

Logging

This is a system where children can record their own activities and attitudes to those activities and reflect upon their learning periodically. The logs can begin by being structured: children could note what work they did, how long they spent on it, whether they found it easy/hard, fun/boring, what they think they learnt from it, whether they want more of the same or to move on. Parents and teachers can add written comments and suggestions so that the log becomes a joint record of responses to the children's needs.

By reading such logs the teacher can keep in touch with the children without the management problems of conferencing. The log can also be used as the basis for conferencing.

For younger children, the process of self-analysis can be done orally, or by letting the children colour the face which shows how they feel (for example, in a continuum from fun to boring), or the picture which shows whether they want something easier, the same, harder, or quite different (for example, pictures of children playing on different rungs of the ladder on the climbing frame or on a different piece of apparatus such as the swings).

Mapping/modelling

This is a procedure whereby the child draws a diagram or 'map' of the main aspects of what they think they have learnt and how the pieces fit

31

together. It is best done at the end of a topic or section of study and can be used to record the facts/concepts/ideas and their relationships.

Information from the above methods can be recorded on checklists which itemize possible skills, concepts and attitudes which the children are developing and the level at which they are performing.

Marking

This is a very common way for teachers to monitor a child's learning. However, it is often done in the child's absence (the books are taken home for marking). It is therefore limited to monitoring the end product and is more evaluatory than diagnostic. Nevertheless, if the 'miscues' (mistakes or omissions) are analyzed and a pattern emerges — in that piece of work or over a series of pieces — then future learning/teaching points can be identified.

Testing

There are many different types and purposes of tests and it is important to distinguish their functions and the different ways in which the results can be used. For example, tests can be devised by the teacher which are directly related to the learning experiences of those children, and can be used to assess how much the children have learnt. Tests are also produced by publishers and are intended to be applicable in a wide range of learning situations.

The purposes of the test depend on the kind of 'learning' which it is intended to test. This can be seen in terms of what the children have remembered, what they have understood and how they have responded, or whether they can apply and how they use their new knowledge and skills — both cognitive and social.

A range of formats are required to match these different purposes, for example, closed or open, multiple choice, interpretive, problem-solving. Different conditions are needed to be able to give opportunities for a fuller range of learning to be demonstrated, for example, timed or untimed, written or practical, individual or group.

Finally the results can be used to rank children against each other (norm referenced), or to rate individual development against past performance (criterion referenced). Results can be diagnostic, prognostic or simply an evaluation of performance at a particular point in time.

How Can Teachers Help Children to Learn How to Learn?

If we accept that one of the main strengths of topic work is that it allows children to learn how to learn through tasks which they can identify as purposeful and therefore motivating, then we need to focus very particularly on this notion of learning to learn.

Dearden (1976) distinguishes four different aspects of this term: general substantive principles, formal methods of enquiry, self-management skills, and information-finding skills. He suggests that these are a family of second-order, generalizable strategies which have high first-order, practical application. It is the last of these with which the remainder of this chapter is concerned.

Information Skills

Again, we can distinguish a number of related terms which overlap: life skills, study skills, library skills, information skills. It is the last term which we will use here. For the purposes of this book we will use information skills to mean:

(a)   identifying the information that is wanted
       — posing the questions;
(b)   selecting possible sources of information
       — primary   (oral/visual/experiential)   and   secondary (maps/documents/books);
(c)   locating the information
       — primary, for example, designing survey/observation schedule setting up the test conditions;
       — secondary, for example, using library catalogue using contents and index;
(d)   extracting and recording information
       — choosing a reading strategy appropriate for the purpose;
       — using a variety of recording techniques/media;
(e)   interpreting/integrating/interrogating information
       — checking accuracy, adequacy;

(f) presenting findings
  — audio/video recording;
    pictorial/graphic/numerical records (2-D, 3-D, IT);
    verbal written/oral presentations.

Each of these areas can be associated with particular attitudes, strategies and skills which together contribute to a positive approach to learning and to knowledge of how to learn. The components of such an approach, in order to become positive for both children and teachers, need to made explicit and to be discussed in a language which is common and meaningful to all concerned.

One of the first issues concerns the difference between using fiction books and non-fiction. Children are familiar with fiction. It is the type of book with which most of them learnt to read. It is often the only kind of book which they are taught how to read. Recent HMI and Schools Council reports (DES, 1978 and 1979) have found little evidence for the teaching of reading skills in the content areas. Yet a different approach to reading such books is needed (Harri-Augstein *et al*, 1982). This involves particular attitudes and reading strategies to meet the particular types of problems which the different style of text poses. Additional strategies are also needed to match the different purposes for which such books are read.

Attitudes

It is most important to encourage an interactive rather than a receptive approach to books of all types. The receptive approach to 'topic' work is all too evident in the type of written presentation where there is considerable copying from books in what appears to be an attempt 'to find out all about...' or, a 'collectomania' approach. This approach often shows little evidence of children having considered what they wanted to find out or why. There is little evidence, therefore, of the child engaging in much thinking or having 'made it their own'.

An interactive approach, by contrast, requires considerable think-ing BEFORE any reading takes place in order to 'orientate' the reader. This can be done by asking such questions as:

What do I already know about this topic?
What more do I want to know?
Which of these aspects might this book help me to answer?

If children list specific questions first, it will help to focus their attention and to read more purposefully and selectively.

An interactive approach also requires thinking DURING reading. This relates to particular 'expectations' which need to be encouraged. Children should expect to:

Check findings against their own/other's experience and books.
Make inferences, read between the lines, make judgments.
Raise further questions for subsequent follow-up.

Further, it would be helpful to encourage children to check the likely accuracy of the information, for example:

When was the book written?
Why — any bias?

Reading Strategies

As children begin to read different kinds of writings and to read them for different purposes, it is useful to encourage them to adopt a range of reading strategies, so they can adopt the strategy most suited to their purpose (Harri-Augstein *et al*, 1982). These might include:

skimming:	very rapid glance to gain overall impression and check if this section is useful;
scanning:	looking for particular points, names, numbers to pick out specific items;
steady read:	to take in content at a general level to provide background especially if new subject;
stop-go:	an interrupted read to enable the reader to stop take notes, check understanding, skip on to next section etc.

Text Characteristics

Recent research has helped to identify some of the differences between fiction and non-fiction which cause problems for some children (Perera

1984). These include:

	FICTION	**NON-FICTION**
STYLE	Personal	Impersonal
	Everyday language	Specialist register
SUBSTANCE	People, situations	Concepts, processes
	Descriptions, feelings	Analytic, objective
STRUCTURE	Redundency, elaboration	Precise, concise
	— simple	— embedded
	— subject introduced at beginning of sentence	— modifying phrases before subject
SHAPE	Chronological development	Logical development
	— story leads to climax	— little excitement

The boundaries between fiction and non-fiction are not always clear cut, in terms of the above features. For example, 'narrative information' books are a category of non-fiction books which have emerged to try to overcome some of the difficulties of the traditional 'text' book. These are written in a 'story' style, yet include a high level of information. This is particularly appropriate to describing the 'life cycle' of animals and plants. It has also been applied to the 'story' of how a river develops, how potato crisps are made and many other processes. Biography/autobiography also uses many of the characteristics of fiction. Perhaps these are good reasons for the popularity of topics, particularly with infant children, such as 'famous people', 'the job of a ...' and 'animal studies'.

Text Style and Layout

Children experience difficulties — or can be helped — through a number of stylistic features: text structure, introduction or context, connectives and cohesion, contiguity, sentence structure and vocabulary. They can also be helped by the way the text, and illustrations, are laid out on the page. Each of these will be examined.

(i) Recent research has suggested that children need to be helped to recognize 'expository text type' and to look at the whole before examining the intricate parts (Meyer, 1984). This means scanning a passage to identify which category of text it is:

'because' type (causative);
'if-then' or 'so that' type (problem/solution);
'this-that' type (comparative);
'all about...' type (descriptive);
'this sort of group' type (collective/classificatory).

An example of each of these is given below, in a simplified single sentence such as might be found in an advertising slogan.

I switched to using KAT LIT because my son said, 'Get rid of that smell or get rid of the cat' (causative).
Our cat's tray smelt, so I tried KAT LIT (problem/solution).
KAT LIT keeps down the smells; other lits don't (comparative).
KAT LIT is clean, economical and easy to use (descriptive).
A good lit is one which de-odorizes and is economical (classificatory).

Meyer suggests that the order given above is in ascending order of difficulty — chronological, narrative type text being easier than any of the above expository texts. However, identifying the 'type' of text is not always easy, but if children can be encouraged to do this, it helps them to predict the way information will be presented and what they can expect to find. The element of prediction is an important contributory factor to understanding.

The suggestion to examine the whole text first is in direct contrast with the traditional approach to comprehension which encourages readers to examine the text for details, often at a literal level. Instead, research is now urging us to approach a text more wholistically and then to refine our detailed understandings afterwards. (This is also in keeping with recent trends of learning to read fiction books, where the emphasis is on first enjoying the whole story and on reading 'real' books.)

(ii) A second aspect which helps children to tackle text is to encourage them to look for the general context, or introduction, which serves to orientate the reader. This also helps the reader to predict what will follow. Well-structured text may summarize the main 'keys' or points to be made either at the beginning (deductive) or at the end (inductive). In order to lead the reader through what follows, changes in direction in the text will often be introduced by 'signal' words which can alert the reader to a change of key or shift in the information. Words such as 'and', 'also', 'in addition', 'further' are considered to be 'additive' signals; 'but', 'however', 'nevertheless', 'whilst', signal 'adversative' (alternative or modifications); 'like', 'as — as', 'similarly' signal 'analogies'.

(iii) A further feature of text which is important in helping the reader is the extent to which the connections between sentences are made explicit. These 'cohesive' links have been identified as being by repetition of same or similar words, or reference to key ideas often through the use of pronouns. They can be linked through forward-acting (cataphoric) or backward-acting (anaphoric), by ellipsis (inferred) substitutions or conjunctions (Chapman, 1987).

The more links that can be traced through the text (like a path through a maze) the more cohesion there is in the text and easier it is to understand. However, a familiar feature of many 'simple' information books is to leave out the details — and often the reasons (or other links) within and between sentences. For example,

> In Tudor London the population grew rapidly. The streets were very dirty and the houses unclean. Many young children died. People from the countryside often came to live in the towns.

There are no explicit links offered between these sentences — they are not cohesive: there are no examples of repetition, reference etc. The information appears arbitrary, disconnected and therefore harder to remember — and less worth remembering.

Another feature of text is the way in which details in the text follow on in a predictable and non-arbitrary fashion i.e.

whether the subject and predicate is contiguous (Bransford *et al*, 1984). For example,

> The huge crane is red .... is non-contiguous
> The huge crane is powerful .... is contiguous

(iv) A further text factor relates to vocabulary, in particular the familiarity of the words used and the frequency of any new words which come from a 'specialist' register. Even if such specialist words are needed children can be helped by being given a definition or example within the text itself, either before the word is introduced or afterwards, in parenthesis. Specialist words can be supported typographically in emboldened type face, or included in a glossary. They can also be supported visually by a picture or labelled diagram. Having once been introduced, the specialist words can be reinforced through repeated use.

Although frequency is important another aspect of vocabulary is the density of concepts, or the number of different ideas presented in close proximity. This is sometimes measured by a 'noun count' in a sentence or passage. Again, the reader can be helped verbally, through examples and elaboration in the text, as well as visually.

(v) Finally, text layout can contribute to helping the reader. In particular,

> the density of print on the page;
> the typeface used;
> the quantity, quality of illustrations within the text;
> the relationship between text and illustration;
> the purpose of illustrations: scene-setting/specific focusing.

The importance of understanding WHAT makes a text difficult lies in the fact that it can help us to devise strategies for HOW we can help the child. General strategies often fall into one of three categories:

(a) avoidance of text by delivering information orally and relying solely on first-hand experiential learning;

(b) bridging the gap by simplifying the text so that children can gain confidence before tackling harder ones, by structuring questions which will help to guide the reader through the text, by explicitly discussing the difficulties and identifying supportive strategies;

(c) constructive criticism of the offending texts by the children, teachers and parents to the publishers.

Each of these approaches can have a part to play in helping children. They need to be used selectively and purposefully to suit the particular child, book and situation.

Recording Techniques

Apart from these activities which take place BEFORE and DURING reading, there are also a set of activities which can take place AFTER the reading. This relates to a range of recording techniques. As a general principle, readers can be encouraged to read, cover, note key words, sequence, fill out into phrases and finally check for accuracy. Younger readers will probably need to read with an adult and the key words and phrases discussed orally and perhaps written by the adult.

It has been suggested that many young children (and adults) are 'visualizers' rather than 'verbalizers'. This means that a reader may find it easier to 'read' more visual forms of information such as diagrams, maps, flow charts, tables, time–lines, attribute webs etc. than to take in information from large chunks of consecutive prose. It has also been suggested that an effective way to 'test' comprehension is to encourage the reader to 'translate' the information from one medium to another i.e. from verbal to visual or vice versa (Lunzer and Gardner, 1984; Sheldon, 1986). Certainly, this could be one way of stopping the copying that has been found to be a feature of some topic work. Children could be encouraged to represent different types of text in different ways. For example:

TEXT TYPE	VISUAL REPRESENTATION
Describing (single items)	Attribute webs, labelled diagram
Locating	Map, plan
Sequential/ordering	List, time–line
Classifying (many items)	Venn diagram, tree diagram
Comparing	Table, matrix, pie–chart
Cause-effect	Networks, flow-chart.

Identifying the text type is not, of course, always easy. Nevertheless, it could be an important extension of children's recording skills for them to be encouraged to experiment with such alternative 'modelling' and 'mapping' techniques.

Support Strategies

A recent experiment in a top junior class resulted in the children themselves, identifying problems which had emerged for many of them during their separate group investigations. Many of these related closely to the nine questions suggested by Marland (1981) as a guide to information skills. After discussing their problems together they devised 'Help' cards to suggest ways round the difficulties.

One of the main problems which the children identified was that of 'getting started'. Having chosen a 'topic', children can be invited to 'brainstorm' and to either list any words or phrases which they associate with the chosen key word (topic) or to pose questions to which they would like to find answers. The words and questions can be arranged in a 'web' to show how they relate to each other and how the ideas develop.

This can be summarized in 'Help' cards:

Getting Started - Have a Brainstorm!

Take a clean piece of paper.
Write down your key topic word.
What does this key word remind you of ...
Jot down any other words that 'go with' the key ...
Can you link any of them together into a web?

Any Questions?

Note down what you already know about any of the word-ideas you have got.
Which of these ideas would you like to find out more about?
List your questions. See if a friend has any to add.
Try asking WHO, WHAT, WHERE, WHY, HOW, WHEN...

Choosing Where To Start

Look at your questions.
Do any of them ask nearly the same thing?
Do any of them 'go together'?
Try to SORT and group the ideas.

Look at each group of ideas.
Try to SPECULATE or guess the answers.
Are some questions more interesting than others?
Are some questions more important than others?
Does the answer to one question help you to answer another
    one?
Try to SEQUENCE your questions, put them in order.

Having got started, and decided 'what I want to find out' the next question is 'where can I find what I want'. It is important for children to be encouraged to use a wide range of sources and to learn to assess which sources would be the most use for which kinds of information. Books, for example, may not be the best source. Alternative sources include observation, experimentation, asking, making a written request, using specific artifacts. These include primary and secondary sources as well as sources which could be found in the classroom or school, in the home, within a mile of the school, five miles, a day-trip away or perhaps from abroad. Again, the children could summarize some of these alternatives in a 'Help' card:

Where To Go For an Answer?

Do you want facts, feelings or opinions.
Which of these would help you most?

Look around you, in the classroom or outside.
Is the answer something you could see?
Look in the Library.
Is the answer something you could read?
If you can't look it up, ask or write to someone.
Write to an expert ...
If you want other's views or experiences, then
Design an interview, questionnaire or survey ...

If books are the most useful source, using them effectively can be very difficult. Locating the book or the section within a book depends on the way information is classified. This can cause great difficulty on many occasions. Library subject categories and key words in an index are usually of a more general nature than the very specific questions that children ask. This means that a child has to be able to think laterally and to understand the links which might situate their question within a different context. Such classification problems require a large vocabulary as well as flexibility of classification. A further 'Help' card gave some suggestions.

Finding Useful Books and Information

Which Library section will be most useful?
  Check the subject index.
Which part of the book will be most useful?
Check the Contents and Index.
Try to think of other key words which mean almost the same
  thing, or, which might also be linked.

Another problem is knowing how to extract and handle the information. Children frequently adopt a 'collectomania' approach to information. They 'lift' it, copy it, even enjoy it, but they often don't actually work on it and make it their own. If we wish children to become critical users of information rather than just sponges, it is important that they are encouraged to look for patterns: similarities/differences, cause/effect, continuity/change, facts/feelings/beliefs. They also need to expect and look for inconsistencies between texts.

Information books for primary children frequently don't provide the level of detail which children soon begin to demand. In such instances, children can be encouraged to read the pictures and diagrams from books where the text is 'hard'. Additionally, parents or other 'better' readers can be asked to help by reading them to the individual child, or even by making a tape of the relevant section which can be added to the library resources.

Where the information is difficult to find, children can be encouraged to speculate on the possible 'answer'. This could encourage them to think for themselves and to learn to value their own and each other's ideas.

A useful technique which can help to discourage 'collectomania' is to suggest that children translate information which they may find in verbal form into visual/graphic form, for example, tables, charts, flow diagrams (as outlined above). Conversely, if the information is already in visual form the children can translate it into a verbal form. This puts an end to copying and ensures that the child has had to act upon the information. It can also encourage a more critical, interactive approach to reading.

Such strategies can be summarized in the next set of 'Help' cards:

How To Record Your Information?

Look at your questions. Remind yourself about what you are
   trying to find out.
If you are comparing things, would it help to make a chart/
   table ...
If you want to describe something, would it help to draw a
   diagram/map ...
If you want to list events/changes, would it help to make a time
   line ...

How To Make Sense of What You've got?

Check if you have all the answers you wanted.
Try asking HOW, WHEN, WHAT, WHERE, WHEN, WHY,
   SO WHAT
Do you need to ask any new questions?
Do any of your answers seem to contradict?

Compare your answers. Look for PATTERNS.
   Do any answers seem to 'go together'?
Examine your findings. Look for REASONS.
   Does any answer help to explain another?

Having collected and sorted the findings, the next step is to present them and share them with the intended audience.

How To Present the Findings?

Decide what you want to say. Make headings.
Decide who you are going to say it to ...
    what age, how many ...
Decide how you want to share your findings.
Try listing the advantages/disadvantages of each
    tape recording, or video
    poster, picture, cartoon strips
    model, pop-up book, zig-zag book
    play, mime, dance
    quiz cards, make-your-own-adventure book
    loose-leaf folder, bound book.

Finally, it is often helpful for the whole class to meet together periodically to discuss their own progress and to ask for advice from each other. Problems relating to information skills are often common between groups, even though the content of their investigations may be very different. Such opportunities can help to make the learning processes public and therefore available for examination and discussion — thus developing the common language and heightening awareness of the 'metacognitive' strategies. Hence children can learn to share and share to learn.

In Conclusion

The points raised in part 1 are intended as an initial framework for analyzing how we might set about 'doing topic work'. There is no inherent value in any given set of variables or criteria. The value is in responding to them and generating your own.

Part 2:
Topic Work in Action

Introduction

The eight case-studies in part 2 include examples from across the whole primary age range and across all the content areas of the curriculum. The case-studies also illustrate different organizational contexts — individual, group and class — and also different types of topic work — interest-based, concept-based and problem-solving.

Despite the many differences, there are a number of common threads.

First, all the case-studies demonstrate children's capacity for taking responsibility for planning and developing topic work themselves. In doing this they become more involved, more motivated and the learning is in a real context which is meaningful for them.

Secondly, many of the case-studies demonstrate the importance of encouraging the children to focus the investigations purposefully by asking specific questions to which they want to find the answers.

Thirdly, in sharing this responsibility with the children, the teachers found it important to allow time for the children's ideas to incubate, for mistakes to be made, critical discussion to follow and for further planning to occur.

Fourthly, despite the emphases on different content areas the main focus is on the learning process and in particular on the awareness of the transferable skills and strategies which the children develop i.e. extracting, recording, using and presenting information.

Finally, discussion and constant critical evaluation throughout the topic work is seen as a vital way of engaging the children in their own learning. By this means they learn to identify and articulate issues related to learning and become aware of the strategies they have used to help them to learn how to learn.

Chapter 3:
Following the Snail Trail

Margaret Armitage

In 'Following the Snail Trail' we see an example of where Infant children took a great deal of the control and responsibility for the topic into their own hands. The topic was shaped according to the questions they posed and the investigations they undertook.

This chapter also illustrates some of the many problems the children faced when using information books and planning experiments. Margaret Armitage describes the way she and her class met those challenges and how, together, they devised a number of strategies to support each other in locating, extracting and recording information.

The topic described in the following pages was undertaken at the beginning of the school year, with a class of 6-year-old top infants. The school is a group 4 primary school on the outskirts of Oxford city and the children come from a variety of social backgrounds. Before the start of the term I had decided upon specific aims and objectives for the topic work I intended to do — both long- and short-term.

My aims were to:-

1   Facilitate a range of learning experiences (pairs, small groups) in order to develop social skills and relationships between individuals in the new class.
2   Observe how far the children were able to take on the responsibility for planning, organizing and evaluating whatever investigation was decided upon.
3   Promote enjoyment in tackling problems cooperatively through questioning, estimating, predicting and testing.

4   Develop any opportunities for first-hand experience and exploration.

My Objectives were to:-

1   Develop oral skills:
   (i)   discussion and constructive criticism in pairs, groups and class situations;
   (ii)   hypothesizing and predicting;
   (iii) explaining and describing a sequence of events.

2   Develop listening skills:
   (i)   identifying key ideas and meanings;
   (ii)   becoming aware of others' points of view and their value as individuals;
   (iii) allowing time and space for the children to consider other's ideas.

3   Develop writing skills:
   (i)   making simple notes;
   (ii)   presenting information/ideas/questions etc. in a variety of ways;
   (iii) encouraging an awareness of a variety of audiences;
   (iv)   simply increasing confidence to write and put marks on paper without always asking how a word is spelled;
   (v)   supporting inventive spelling thus enabling assessment of the child's concepts of words and letters;
   (vi)   drafting and redrafting.

4   Develop reading skills:
   (i)   identifying and locating a variety of resources;
   (ii)   using the subject classification system in the schools reference library;
   (iii) using a simple index and contents page;
   (iv)   locating main ideas;
   (v)   presenting new knowledge in a graphic form;
   (vi)   possible introduction to graphic cues i.e. headings, underlining, heavy print etc. to encourage flexibility of approach and rates of speed in reading.

From Spirals to Snails

Usually the children themselves are the sources of inspiration for specific topics and these act as vehicles for the promotion of my objectives. However, the start of a new school year is always tricky.

It is difficult to know how to stimulate discussion on that first morning. What kind of display would contain a variety of possibilities for further development and be likely to encourage the aims and objectives I had selected?

Often the children bring in shells from their holidays, so I decided to set up a display of objects which had a spiral pattern — a corkscrew, a spring, twisted birthday candle etc. It was hoped that this might promote discussion as to why such diverse objects were on the same display and that the children's observations of similar patterns in the environment might be extended. The children themselves would make the connections. In the meantime, my role was to consider all the possibilities which might be developed from the display, both in terms of practical activities and in curriculum matters. Just as important was the need to observe and listen to the children as they handled the objects, because from these observations the actual focus of our work would develop.

For several days, the original spiral display had been growing rapidly as the children found objects with a similar pattern. Their acute observation was astounding and parents were also becoming involved in the hunt for spirals. Even the quiet book time at the beginning of the afternoon session became the time to search through books to find anything remotely resembling a spiral shape.

Then, two exciting discoveries were made which set the course for the rest of the term. One child found pictures of snails in a book. She showed the class and the book was proudly added to the display. After playtime, on the same day, many children came back into the classroom excitedly clutching handfuls of very tiny (and apparently empty) snail shells which had been found in various areas of the playground. Soon the warmth of the room stimulated the 'empty' shells into life! Within half an hour, the majority of the miniature snails brought in after play were crawling all over the spiral collection. This was a vital time for me to listen to the children's questions and comments in order to assess their level of knowledge for example,

Slugs are snails without shells.
These are grown up snails 'cos they've got shells.
What's that white stuff on my hand?
Those long things on their head are for feeling with.

Then came the question:

Can we keep them?

It would have been so easy for me to say 'Yes, of course' and then spend lunchtime looking for information about setting up a vivarium and have it all prepared for the snails, in the afternoon. However, I was determined to stand back and allow the children to take on this task since it was potentially so full of real learning opportunities. Instead I said 'But do you know what to put them in so they will be happy and what about feeding?' A few suggestions were made, but it was obvious nobody had any positive knowledge to give. They appealed to me but I knew no more about snails than they did. Reluctantly, a corporate decision was made: the snails would be returned to their homes until the children had found out about the conditions snails needed in which to live and we had set up a home for them in the classroom.

Asking Questions

At this stage, much of the work was approached through whole class discussions. It was from these sessions that I hoped small groups would form naturally to develop particular aspects of the investigation. We began with the questions asked during the first moments of discovery and discussed how we could find solutions.

Many children were eager to provide the answers immediately even though some of these were contradictory. My aim was to help the class towards locating sources of information and to find a way of organizing what precisely we wanted to know. Thinking about the intermediate stages between question and answer was difficult and it was only through gently challenging many of the children's assumptions that they began to see further detailed research was required. We discussed how we could record our immediate problems.

The following chart was compiled by three children. During the next few days, other small groups filled in any spaces they could (see photograph 1).

The questions we have asked	Where shall we go to find the answer	The answer to the question
How to look after them?	School reference library Holton Park Library	
How to feed them?	Where shall we go to find out — ask Simon, spy on them to copying them (sic)	
Where shall we get them?	Ask each otch (sic)	Looking in at (sic) gardens under things in dark places.
Who shall collect them?		
Wot (sic) to put them in? etc.	Look in a book	

Four main learning aspects were evident in this activity for the children:

(i) The group working on the second column for question 2 obviously felt the need to repeat the column heading 'where shall we go to find the answer?'. The children were unfamiliar with this coordinate-type of format and saw the heading as applying to the first question only.

(ii) The list of questions as written on the chart was not in any logical sequence. It was in the subsequent use of this chart that the children realized for themselves the error.

(iii) The various groups identified a variety of resources — books, own observations/experiences, each other and knowledgeable friends.

(iv) They experienced the challenge of tackling the spelling of new words.

For future development of similar activities, two particular points were noted. First, it would have been advantageous to encourage the children to write their questions on pieces of paper (rather than directly on the chart). This would have made it easier to sort them into logical groups before being stuck on the chart. Secondly, the third column did not leave sufficient room for full information. We had to adopt a 'follow the green string' approach which connected the answer column to a graphic representation of the required information on another section of the display wall.

Locating and Using Resources

This proved to be a very busy and stimulating period. Children were involved in:

— researching the school's reference library using a subject classification system;
— writing to the local schools library service to ask if they could go and find some books about snails;
— booking the use of the minibus for the visit;
— sorting out which children would go to Holton Park Library;
— it was decided at this point that the fairest way would be to organize a half day visit to a local nature reserve to find and study snails. Each child should decide which visit s/he preferred;
— writing letters to parents informing them which visit their children would be involved in and how much it would cost;
— collecting 'trip money' and keeping records of who had paid. Calculators were used to check the amount of money required with the amount collected in.

Towards the end of the week, various groups were formed (mainly on interest and friendship criteria) to begin researching the collected material. It was vital at this stage to ensure each group knew exactly for what information it was seeking. Without that clarity of purpose, much of the skill-getting and skill-using which I hoped the activity would develop, would have been wasted. If the children knew their area to be researched, then the use of contents and index pages, alphabetization, graphic cues and key words/main ideas would have a real context and might avoid the 'finding out about snails' approach resulting in a general muddle of unrelated information.

Organization was now of primary concern. I needed to be able to work with these groups so that I could assess informally the children's present stage of development in the focus skills I had previously identified. I could then use this information to devise future activities. A number of craft activities were also begun at this time which were based on the spiral/snail shape. A good proportion of the class could work independently on these, whilst others were continuing with compilation of charts, posters and personal reading. This released me to give more support to those groups needing help on other aspects.

The visit to Holton Park Library was a very valuable experience. A young librarian welcomed the children and talked briefly about how a library organizes its stock. She helped the children to use the Dewey Classification Index to find the relevant number for 'snails' and the search began. They were encouraged to note all available graphic cues. Each child selected a book and on the journey home, prepared to show and justify his/her selection to the rest of the class.

As children came to the collected material to find possible solutions to the original questions, several skills were required:

— comparing book titles and cover illustrations with the actual material and information which was inside. It soon became clear that some books had been selected solely on the criteria that there was a picture of the snail on the front cover or on an inner page when, in fact, the subject was totally unrelated to snails. The group's first task was to sort the books into a 'no-good' pile and a 'good' pile.

— using flexible reading strategies in scanning a page for informative ideas and useful pictures and in skimming through a book to assess its appropriateness in relation to the question being researched by the group.

— not only using index and contents pages but to see their value in speeding up the process of finding an answer.

— devising ways of making sure useful books/pages are remembered, for example, one group had set out to record on a list the book and page number to be used again. But towards the end of the session, the actual writing process began to become tedious:

> *Th.* There's lots about what to keep them in in this book.
>
> *S.* I don't want to write mine down any more.
>
> *Th.* I could make markers and put them in the pages we want. Then we won't have so much writing to do.

Extracting and Recording Information

Sufficient information had by now been collected to enable us to create a suitable environment for snails. Two, apparently conflicting, descriptions of a vivarium for land snails had been found and provoked a lively discussion as to which plan should be followed. The solution was to make both types and compare the results. The caretaker was invited to help with the actual construction of the boxes and happily took children in twos and threes to the woodwork room to measure, cut and nail the pieces of wood. Two groups of children then used the vivarium plans to create the living areas. Simultaneously, another group decided to keep some pond snails and set about finding the necessary information, drawing a clear sequential plan for construction, and collecting snails from the school pond.

Despite all this activity, we still had no land snails in the class and the children were beginning to get impatient. However, nobody knew really how to look after them and yet I wanted to defer the moment of collection until we were in a position to care for them correctly. A group was given the responsibility to find the information required to answer the question 'How to look after them?'.

In the subsequent evaluation of this particular activity with an experienced, senior colleague, it was clear that without her professional expertise in encouraging, questioning hasty assumptions and redirecting false paths, the children would have been unable to fulfil the allotted task. The skills required included:

— picking out main ideas;
— paraphrasing;
— recording information in a short form, for example, notes of key points using sequence of pictures, charts, diagrams etc;
— scanning page for particular words to help with the writing task;
— checking information from more than one source;
— integrating information from more than one source;
— realizing more than one source can give the same information even when the exact same words are not used.

The children had difficulties in reading the text as there was no independent reader in the group. Some of the information was presented in complex grammatical constructions and was difficult to extract. The text needed breaking into very small chunks for discussion, before the children could come to terms with the information and put it in their own words.

It was felt that these difficulties of extracting and recording could have been largely avoided if the questions the children were asking had been simpler — and answerable in almost one word: for example, Do they need water? Do they need leaves? How often does the box need cleaning? etc. Also, the information gleaned could have been written on separate sentence cards. This would have enabled the children to physically move them around, locate key words/phrases, cut out unnecessary words and organize ideas so that eventually notes could be made rather than wanting to copy chunks from the book.

Another way around the problem soon emerged which helped children who had difficulty in extracting information from the books. An able reader was found who agreed to read relevant pages on to a tape. This provided a real purpose in reading. The less confident readers were also keen to join in: many of them took books home — thus involving the parents too — in order to practice before taping. Each tape was then put into a plastic bag with the book. The children then labelled each bag with a subject title, the title, author and page of the book, and the name of the reader. The tape could then be listened to and the text followed by any child wanting to know about that aspect. The tape could be stopped and replayed as many times as the child wanted in order to find the information they needed (see photographs 7, 8).

A further problem was experienced in trying to discriminate between and assess the value of different sources of information. For example, children researching where to find snails discovered the following discrepancies:-

D: This one says dark and damp.
L: That's wrong. This says cool and shady.
K: Yeah. That book's wrong. It's different.

Later, in the same discussion...

Th: You know those books, 'cool and shady' and the one that said 'dark and damp' ... It's not really wrong. There's a picture here of a stone in a cool and shady place. And underneath, it's all dark and damp. So it's the same really.

Although the text often posed problems diagrams were sometimes easier to interpret. This was found to be the case for two children researching 'diseases'. The children 'read' and discussed a relevant diagram and then decided to write their own, easier, text. This required sequencing information, and constructing simple descriptions so others could easily understand. So, having read the diagram and understood the key concepts the children explained in their own words what it was about. Their interpretations were written down and typed on a jumbo typewriter. The resulting descriptions were straightforward but in reading it through the children discovered they had used too many 'the's'. They altered some to 'then' or 'after that'. The final draft was typed up but, unwittingly, there were errors made such as missing a space between two words, reversal of words (on/no), spelling errors (people/peolpe) and omission of full stops. The children were given the task of proof-reading the text. One of the pair was an independent reader, so he easily found the mistakes — a task which he thoroughly enjoyed. Errors were erased by his partner and corrected with a felt tip pen. It was a novel experience to 'mark' an adult's piece of work — an activity with genuine learning potential.

Another issue which emerged from using information books was the need for note-taking. Some found this idea mystifying. The children frequently believed one book to be adequate and therefore that additions or changes in the information extracted would not be needed. Hence, they preferred to 'take notes' in the intended final form and to write in full sentences. One group, when asked if they would like to think of a way to take notes which would be shorter suggested 'We could write smaller ...' Clearly, the purpose of making notes was not obvious.

It was necessary, with some of the children, to write down their 'notes' for them. In this way, they were introduced, orally, to the technique of saying something in a shorthand manner by locating key words and phrases and omitting words like 'the' and 'a'. Similarly, the task of describing orally what had been heard on the tape helped to internalize the information given. The resulting record reflected the child's own language and understanding instead of being copied from a book or a tape.

The above technique was used when a child wanted precise details which were embedded in a tape or in a text. For example, when a child wanted to discover more about 'mating' or 'growing', s/he was encouraged to break down the subject into more manageable questions for which one word answers would be required. By this method, scanning skills through the auditory and visual senses were developed i.e. listening for key words and ideas. When the necessary piece of information was found it needed to be noted down. For some of the children the writing task was eased by the use of an adult to ensure that the real purpose of the task (extracting information to fulfil a previously defined goal) would not become marred by the mechanical process of writing.

One aspect which developed from the use of tapes which I had not foreseen was that of developing the writing style of those children who were able to write their own summaries. It was not copying, but they definitely developed a more literary style, using longer and more complex sentences with a greater flow than before.

Apart from writing, the children were encouraged to present the information in a number of different ways. For example:

— a chart showing all relevant points about caring for snails with illustrations to aid the reading;
— on this chart, the children used √ and X to indicate the do's and don'ts;
— the use of ditto marks was discovered and used enthusiastically;
— a 3D chart to show which foods were to be given to the snails each day;
— a pictorial representation of the proposed 'homes' using their own ideas of labelling (one group devising a quite sophisticated colour-coded key) to show the required layers of soil, peat, leaf mould etc.

One of the problems, for the teacher, which emerged was the dilemma between skill-getting and skill-using. Which should come first? Finding out about using books got in the way sometimes of finding out about snails and without the sympathetic support of patient, clear sighted adults, the enthusiasm of the children might have waned. Yet I strongly believe the acquisition of skills must have its roots in activities which are relevant, realistic and important to the child. If the learner sees the purpose of acquiring a useful skill and, with help, begins to utilize it in a self-determined context, then the teacher can devise similar experiences in which the skill can be practiced. Only by this approach do I think we can encourage the transfer of learning across the curriculum and in different situations (see photographs 9–14).

Refining and Sorting Questions and Hypotheses

Search parties set out to find specimens from the school grounds and these were then proudly introduced to their new 'homes'. A rota system was devised with the children so that two of them would be responsible for the care of the snails on a weekly basis.

It was tempting at this stage to organize experiments on such aspects as movement, eating and smelling which I had read up in science books, but I felt I would then be taking the course of the topic out of the children's hands. By observing and listening, I became aware that the class was not ready yet for such activities and I was determined not to lose sight of my original objective — that of allowing the space and time for the children to develop a project at their natural pace and as their interest in specific aspects was awakened. When a topic is 'pre-packaged' by the teacher before a term starts, it is extremely difficult to allow oneself the luxury of standing back, waiting, and watching. Indeed, I know all too well how annoying it can be if a class seems more interested in an area one has not incorporated into the flow chart! What usually happens is that only those questions which fit in with the ideas on the topic web are focused upon so that other potentially rich investigations are excluded. The teacher needs to be aware of possible developments and activities and to have a clear idea of the purpose of the work undertaken, but such plans must take into account the children's stage of knowledge and interest and be flexible enough to incorporate spontaneous developments.

The other major activity was to sort out the individual questions which the children were listing. The actual questions were cut out to allow the group to physically manipulate them and sort them. This time the skills required were:

— understand the term 'sorting', 'things that go together';
— categorization of ideas;
— achieve corporate decision-making;
— organization of group members;
— choosing ways of presenting the categories in graphic form.

Grouping proved difficult for these children. There seemed to be no clear criteria for putting two questions together rather it was more an association of ideas. For example, 'where is the snails nose?' was grouped with 'how do they feed?' because, according to the children, they both referred to the 'front end of the snail'. Finding a general label, or superordinate, for the groups also proved a struggle but labels for the categories were eventually selected with which the children appeared satisfied.

It was hoped that this particular area of work would form the basis for an introduction to self-evaluation of an activity later in the term after the chart had been used and, perhaps, found to be inaccurate or unsatisfactory by the users (i.e. the children) themselves. What was particularly noteworthy was the form in which the group chose to present their work. Not for them the neatly drawn rows. The members decided to create a spiral chart — commencing in the centre with the questions on 'babies', moving out through 'head parts', 'eating', 'breathing', 'moving', 'growing' to end with 'diseases' and, presumably, death. This was one of the most original, imaginative and creative outcomes of the investigation and did not require any assistance from adult logic.

Several discussions with the whole class had revealed that instead of posing questions which could be answered through observation of physical aspects, the children were now posing such problems as 'which of the snails is the strongest/fastest?', 'when were snails invented?', 'what will snails eat/not eat?' and 'do different types of snail like different types of food?'. Exactly how a test could be set up was discussed by the class so that a variety of ideas could be evaluated by the children. A group was formed to investigate food preferred by snails but, in the early stages, its members had little idea about conducting a fair test.

> Let's put lots of different food and see what they eat.
> But they might not all like the same thing.
> Just have one snail at a time.
> You could have two and put a barrier between them.

A variety of foods was collected and scattered over the stones and leaf mould without any pattern. Some pieces were deliberately hidden or put in awkward places. Even though this group had initially decided to separate the vivarium into two and test the eating habits of two snails, the children made no attempt to create a barrier nor divide the food equally between the snails. Even with questioning, it was clear the group had no framework for observation and could give no justification for the way in which they had set up the experiment. However, no intervention was made at this point. The learning would come if the children themselves recognized the errors. Next day, the group saw that some of the food had gone rotten. Also, they could not be sure if any food had been eaten as they could not recall exactly where it has been placed nor how many pieces had been put in the vivarium. The children concluded that the test was a failure but the reasons which they gave to the class showed mature scientific analysis:

> The snail might not have eaten the food in the corner because it didn't like the corner.
> Perhaps he couldn't see it.
> Or smell it.
> Maybe it was too hard to get ...

Subsequently, a new test was devised. This time, the food was put in a dish which remained in the same position throughout the experiment. A map was made of the snails' position at the start and their movements plotted. At the end of each day, the food was examined to see what had been eaten and any pieces beginning to go off were removed. A pictorial record was made of all food put in and $\sqrt{}$ and X were put against the pictures depending on whether that piece of food had been tasted or not.

When two children wanted to find out how strong snails were by testing how much they could pull, I decided that the learning which had come from the previous experiment should be used to influence the new one. The skills of appreciating the need for controls in a fair test, seeing the need to anticipate the effect of confounding variables and accepting the importance of repeating tests all needed introducing. Again, it was through a lively class discussion that many of these issues were raised.

> *T:* How will you know how much it can pull?
> *K:* See how heavy the stone is.
> *T:* How will you know how heavy it is?
> *AM:* Measure it.
> *K:* Weigh it.
> *T:* How will you do that?
> *K:* Put the stone in on one side (balances) and the snail in the other.
> *T:* Hold on. What do you want to find out? Do you want to know which is heavier, the stone or the snail? Or, do you want to know how heavy the stone is?

T: Let's be sure of what you are going to do. Are you going to use one snail and lots of different stones, or try different snails pulling the same stone?

K: Different snails pulling the same one ...

T: What are you going to do next?

A: Get the snails and the stone.

·T: Both together?

AL: No ... the stones first or the snails might escape.

The discussion ranged over problems of what to put the stone in to help it along the surface, how to attach a harness to the shell and how far the snail had to pull the weight. The vital aspect of concern for the snail's comfort and safety were uppermost in the discussion. These sessions encouraged the children to:

— listen to each other and take turns when speaking;
— contribute ideas and value others;
— generate alternatives and hypotheses;
— provide evidence to justify points;
— challenge ideas and ask questions;
— identify criteria critical to the test;
— consider the ethics of experimentation;
— estimate a reasonable time span for tests.

Beginning to Evaluate

I had decided to make my personal evaluations of the investigation as a whole in the more objective surroundings of the school holiday but I also felt it important that the children were part of this not only because it is a necessary skill to develop from the earlier stages, but because I wished to know what the class's reactions were. Another class discussion session was organized.

Children's Evaluation

(i)   Most rated its success as 4/5 or 3/5 but found it hard to say what they had enjoyed or what they remembered. Many comments were anecdotal — about sitting on some glue, or singing a song while working.

(ii)   Thinking of what they wanted to find out at the start was seen as being 'hard work' but ultimately useful.

(iii)   Using the key on the plans for the snail homes had proved difficult for some — their first experience of this kind of reading.

(iv)   Sequential pictorial diagrams were found easier to use than composite ones.

(v)   The difficulties of sorting and grouping the questions were identified but the children were unable to state precisely what was difficult or how the task could have been approached differently.

(vi)   Similarly, the problems encountered in finding the information were mentioned but the nature of the problems could not be described. What was the difficulty, in fact, was the task of interpreting the language and abstracting the meaning from some of the books.

(vii)   The success of the project was rated mainly in terms of the quantity of knowledge gained rather than in new skills acquired. However, some signs of evaluation of the activities were beginning to show through.

My Own Evaluations

Encouraging topic work of the type described above, where the children take responsibility for the development of the topic, can pose particular challenges for the teacher. Although I had specific aims in mind when I started, inevitably, skills and concepts which were not predicted were required by the children. It is easy to become overwhelmed by the sheer volume of learning activities. This is where the criticism of the undevelopmental, improvised nature of project methods finds its base. Certainly, if one allows the opportunity for children to follow ideas in a flexible environment using the spontaneity of the moment without regard to what has already been experienced or to what would be appropriate to provide for the next stage, then such criticism would be justified. A way of avoiding such pitfalls is:

(i)   select a small number of goals to achieve over a reasonable period of time;

(ii)   select these goals with reference to the children's present level of experience;

(iii)   observe the use of these particular skills;

(iv)   perhaps take note of other skills which were required for future reference but which are not the focus skills;

(v)   concentrate upon the selected skills and record in which activities they were used and evaluate the measure of effectiveness with which they were used;

(vi)   use the collected information to form future goals for the class and for individuals;

(vii)   keep records of individual children's progress to ensure progression of skills at the next stage — assuming that the school has a practical, sequential policy for the teaching of information skills.

In order to keep records of individual progress it assumes that the teacher uses a range of informal assessment techniques in order to monitor the child's learning. Such techniques have the advantage of allowing the teacher to observe the child in the actual learning context so that she can see why errors are made not only the type of mistake. It can also reveal the learner's strengths and weaknesses over a wide variety of activities and with a range of purposes. Therefore, the teacher has a holistic picture of the learner's ability.

However, informal observation of children requires careful planning. It relies on having a simple method of recording observations, a clear idea of what is to be assessed and familiarization with the nature of the task to be undertaken by the child. For example, in the case of reference books, the teacher needs to be aware of any inherent difficulties which might prevent the learner from achieving his goal and to be prepared to help the child through these difficulties without taking the task away from him. This entails planning effective organization of the other children and, where possible, having willing adult helpers which enables the teacher to observe and support a group at work without being interrupted. Such observations have made me aware of how much stamina children have in dealing with problematic resources when they have a real goal in sight.

The information gained from such observations can be used in a number of ways: to plan further practice activities, to modify the learning experiences where necessary and to decide on future priorities.

All of these insights from observing children at work imply a possible shift in teaching approaches if we are to encourage effective, cooperative learning between teacher and children and between the children themselves. For example:

(i)   We need to keep in balance process and product.

(ii)   Encourage the learners to become actively involved in the process through discussion and negotiation.

(iii)   Encourage the learners to become more aware of the value of evaluation and assessment of their own performances.

(iv)   Give greater opportunity for the children to work in small groups without the constraints of adult presence (a) to develop independence and a sense of responsibility; (b) to allow greater freedom for language development within certain boundaries but without adult influence. (Tape recorders can be used as records of the children's work.)

(v)   Allow time for learners to reflect upon and formulate ideas in discussions and to talk to each other in a controlled manner rather than always through the teacher.

(vi)   Encourage independence by spending time discussing and explaining a particular task but then quietly withdrawing.

(vii)   Give the children a model for cooperative learning by one's own behaviour in discussions — encouraging others to express their ideas, giving value to an idea given and by exhibiting how to achieve a consensus of opinion.

(viii) Ensure that learners have a real purpose for their activity and that they have a clear idea of the outcome and the intended audience.

(ix)   Develop the role of the teacher as a guide, working alongside and with the children in the pursuit of well-defined aims.

It is clear that heavy demands will be placed on both teacher and children but, as was evident on the snail trail, the children's excitement, motivation and total involvement will generate all the energy required.

I. Identifying Issues

What do we want to find out?

the questions we have asked	where we can go to find the answer
how to Look after them?	Look in a book School refrence Library
how to feed them? what they like to eat	where we can find the answer Simons friend spy on the snails
how do	

Photograph 1   What do we want to find out? Chart of the children's original questions (see p. 53)

II. Making the Process Public

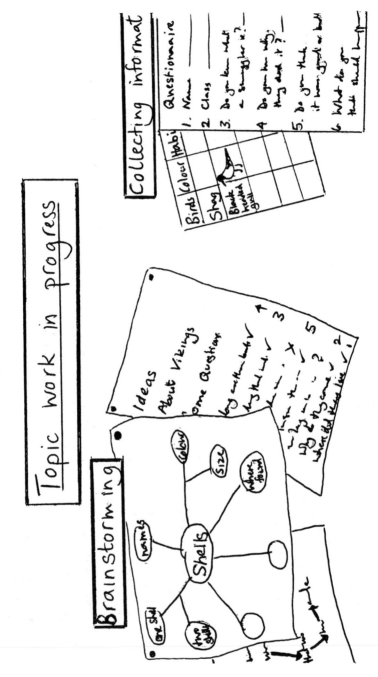

Photograph 2   How we started off — brainstorming — ideas web — list of questions — Collecting data — comparative chart

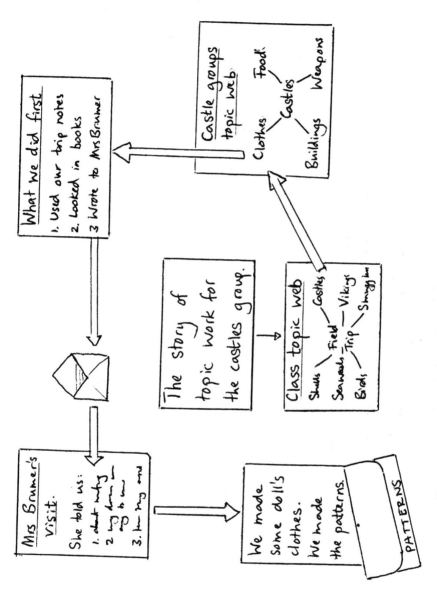

Photograph 3 How the topic developed — links between the sub-groups (see p. 85)

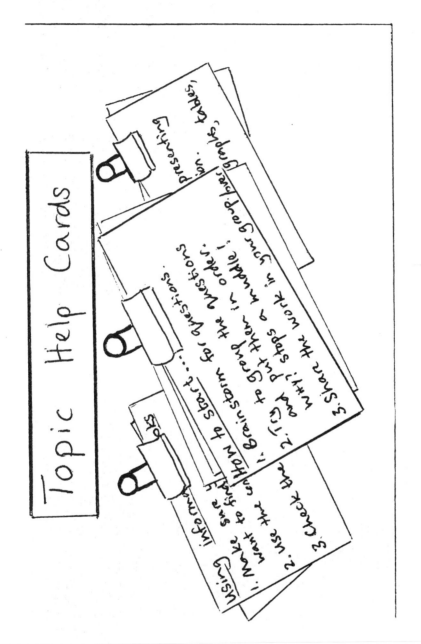

Photograph 4 How we helped each other

III. Locating Information

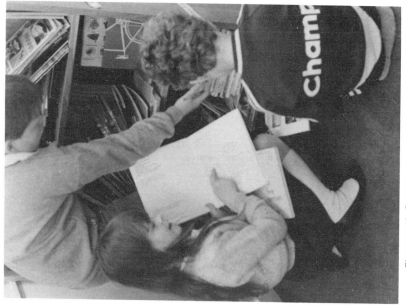

Photograph 5 Using library catalogues (see p. 90)

Photograph 6 Using contents' pages (see p. 90)

Photograph 7 Extracting information aurally from library of information (see p. 57)

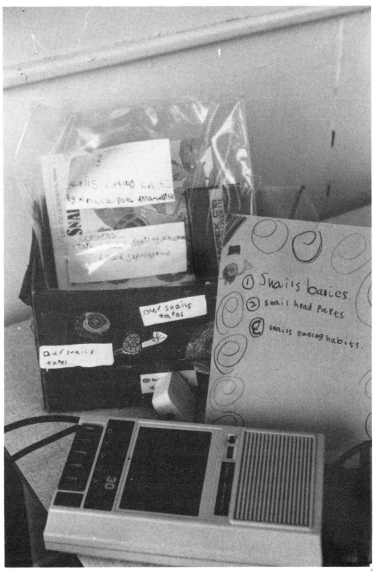

Photograph 8 Tapes made by children (see p. 57)

Chapter 4:
Oh Goody, It's Champagne Again!

Tina Ruff

Introduction

This chapter also shows the value of providing real motivation and a real context for learning. In 'Oh goody, it's champagne again' we see the children taking on much of the responsibility for planning and shaping the direction of the topic. We also see the children experimenting with new ways of extracting and presenting information.

Tina Ruff discusses some of the delights — and the difficulties — in establishing new approaches to topic work, this time with older children with already established study habits.

It all began with a large bottle of champagne, or rather its box propped up against my neighbour's dustbin. Along one side was printed QUADRUPLE MAGNUM. What size bottle is that I wondered? What's it for? How much did it cost? Can I have the empty bottle for school?

When the bottle was empty we were allowed to use it for capacity — you know the kind of thing:

How much does it hold?
How many glasses will it fill?
How many normal bottles are needed to fill it?
How heavy is it empty and full?

The bottle was called a Methusulah. I asked the children to find out what they could about Methusulah. The next day, one boy said that the biggest bottle of champagne was called a Nebuchadnezzar — or so his dad thought. I suggested we write to Moet & Chandon and ask them. Paul did.

Moet & Chandon were very kind. Their reply came quickly and was very helpful. There was a pamphlet about champagne bottles, booklets on champagne making and the growth of the company. There was the promise of a large bottle — a dummy Salmanazar — and posters being sent to us separately, and a casual sentence 'If you or your classmates are ever in France, do come and visit our caves.'

Out of curiosity we looked at a map. Where was Epernay? Was it a long way away? How long would it take to get there? It looked too far for a day trip.

We wondered how big our bottle would be. We borrowed a standard champagne bottle and a Jereboam and measured them. By using their diameter and height we drew a straight line graph. By estimating the increase in diameter for the Salmanazar we read off the prospect of a bottle 70 cms high. That was almost as tall as some of the infants!

A few days later, the postman staggered in with a huge box, which contained a huge bottle. It was our Salmanazar — a twelve bottler!

Table 1: Size and capacity of champagne bottles

Name	Equivalent bottles	Capacity in litres
	1 bottle	.75
Magnum	2 bottles	1.50
Jereboam	4 bottles	3.00
Methusulah	8 bottles	6.00
Salmanazar	12 bottles	9.00
Balthazar	15 bottles	10.25
Nebuchadnezzar	20 bottles	15.00

It was made of glass, not plastic as we had thought. It was about as high as we had estimated, but it was empty! Paul wrote back thanking the company for the bottle and asking more about a trip to the cellars and caves. An enormous poster of the caves added to our interest and in July 1985 we decided we would have to find a way of going to Epernay.

Organizing the Trip

Fortunately the neighbour with the Methusulah was an educational tours operator and planned the trip with us. The cost would be £70 and he suggested the May Bank Holiday weekend of 1986. In September at a meeting with parents I outlined my plans. We would go to the cellars in Epernay, and the children would raise as much of the money as they could for themselves.

Paul wrote again to Moet & Chandon and told them of our intentions. Letters between the company and Paul continued until the visit was over.

There was just seven months for them to raise £70. (The money had to be in a month before we went). We aimed to raise £10 a month for each child. Some of the money they would raise themselves by doing jobs for their families — we emphasized they couldn't go knocking on just anyone's door. We also tried to organize fund-raising efforts for the children in each month.

As the money began to come in, a school post office savings account was opened for each child. From this the children learnt the beginnings of accounting, the need for receipts, and, more importantly to them, about interest. For those who were not used to saving, earning interest was a new and fascinating idea. They quickly realized that their money could earn more money and that to get it in the bank before the end of the month was better than at the beginning of the next — a very real reason for developing mathematical skills!

As an encouragement a pictorial progress was kept around the room. Everyone going was given a cardboard ship, boat, helicopter etc which started at September. As each £10 was added so the vehicle moved on a month. This way we could all see who was keeping up to the target. After Christmas the parents arranged a super raffle which was to be drawn at our French evening. This raised the rest of the money.

Preparing for the Trip: French and France

The fact that we were saving up to go to France provided a very real sense of purpose for all our work. For seven months we thought about France: we thought about the food, the money, the country and the language. I tried to introduce various French phrases into the daily life of the school. Every visitor to the school was asked to contribute to this new-found vocabulary and we tried to speak French whenever we could. Unfortunately none of the obvious contacts were able to supply what we really needed — a French teacher!

Figure 1: Topic web for work on France.

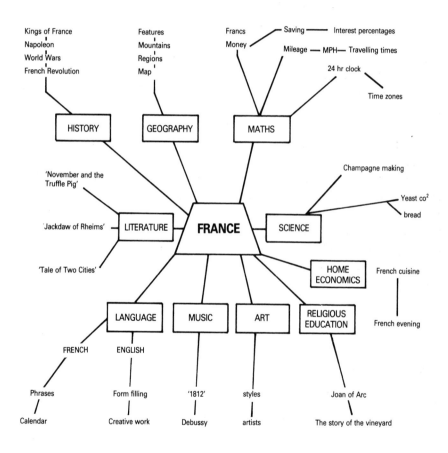

One of the things which fascinated the children about the language was the use of tu and vous. They were intrigued to know that they should be calling me vous, but their parents tu. They were horrified to discover that I should call them tu, just as I did the dog! This lead on to discussion about how, in English, they talked to different people in different ways — and according to what you wanted from them! The children began to identify the differences in how they talked to their grandparents compared to how they talked to their friends. They came to understand about how we use language — about style, register, audience — even if, in England, we do not mark such differences by such obvious methods as tu and vous.

They found gender difficult to grasp as well — why was a window feminine but the sun male? Why were all horses male? Were mares still talked of as male or did they always refer to a female horse as a mare? We talked about other languages — how did the Germans decide what was neither male or female. How did anyone decide that the sea was female?

In the term before we went, it seemed appropriate to find out more about the country and region we were going to. So, I began my planning by drawing up a topic web. My intention was to make sure that every area of the curriculum was covered during the term's work.

From Content to Skills

During the term, my focus for topic work changed. Instead, the introduction and development of certain research and presentation skills became the main focus of my plans. The content became of secondary importance. I wanted to use it as a way of introducing and expanding skills which could be used in other topics.

Extracting Information

The biggest problems, which we all know only too well, were the lack of appropriate resources for the children in all ability and age ranges and also the lack of time. I was lucky and was able to devote a lot more time than many colleagues in other schools may have been able to do, with the full support of the parents.

Table 2: *Skills, theme and source of information*

Presentation Skills	Topic Theme	Source of Information
Cartoon stories	Napoleon	Reference books
	French Revolution	Reference books
	'Jackdaw of Rheims'	Story book
Annotated diagrams	Champagne making	Booklets
	Wine making	Books and practical work
Annotated map	Joan of Arc	Reference books
	Journey to France	Maps and imagination
Writing and following instructions	Form filling	DHSS, passports, etc
	Cooking	Recipe books
Creative work from factual sources i.e.		
Newspaper reporting	'1812' overture	
Radio reporting	World War 1	Reference books
Art work	Styles of painting	
	Pointillism	Reference books and illustrations

Working through the topic themes caused several problems. Sometimes, the only reference material available was too complicated or too old! For example, extracts from encyclopaedias had to be looked at carefully before the children used them to ensure they would be able to gather sufficient information for their purposes. One encyclopaedia's discourse on Napoleon was so long that the main stages in his life were lost through boredom. Other books paid little attention to the whole of his life story and gave too potted a history. Some information books gave too much detail and confused the children. One book in particular referred to Joan of Arc then to the Maid of Orleans. Only the more able readers picked up the fact that they were the same person and, not, as some thought, two girls caught up in the same adventure.

The poorer readers worked as a group to produce their work. With help, they read the relevant passages, or the passages were read to them while they followed in their own books. Phrase by phrase, sentence by sentence, the process was worked out and put into words and pictures the children could understand. The work of the other children proved an invaluable source of explanation and suitable vocabulary.

Presenting Information

The booklets sent by Moet & Chandon proved very useful. Although the language used was a bit difficult in some places, the process of champagne making was clearly explained. Extracting information from the written form and presenting it as a visual sequence of annotated diagrams was the first exercise in the new approach. The children were able to go off on their own and identify the stages of production then try to write descriptions in their own words. This part of the exercise was the most difficult. After all, trying to be precise and succinct is very hard! This form of presentation became known as 'the champagne way' and is still so called even if the child is going to use it to describe the life cycle of a newt.

Enfin

Well, the trip to France was a great success. The tour of the cellars was fascinating. We saw Napoleon's hat, thousands of champagne bottles, toasted Paul with champagne, took pictures of each other outside the cellars and spent our francs in the shop. We spent the afternoon looking for the Jackdaw in Rheims Cathedral and visiting the museums. In fact we did all the things tourists do. The children tried to speak French, but got by well with sign language!

On the way home we went to Canada, well, to the Canadian territory of Vimy Ridge. Under the eagle eye of a French-Canadian guard we were allowed to walk through the trenches where some sixty years before the Canadians had faced the enemy who's trenches seemed so very near. The boys found a rusty gun cemented into place for all to see. The huge bomb craters and the row upon row of trenches are now grassed over and dominated by the grave stones and memorial to all the Canadians who perished there. Even the children were stunned by the thoughts of the horrors of war as we stood in those trenches.

Some of their questions during the trip were totally unexpected. They were also of a very different type — how deep is the channel?; where does the sea go to when the tide turns?; why do the French speak so quickly? Researching and answering these questions would prove difficult. Some could only be met with speculation.

On the return their first memories were of the hotel, of having to ask for their breakfast in French to the Portuguese waitress who spoke little French let alone any English. They recounted their confrontation with some Germans who got over their message by signs(!). Disappointment was expressed by those who did not have their passports even looked at let alone stamped. Quickly, the purpose for our visit faded and became just a small part of an exciting time.

What Had We Actually Learnt From the Topic Work?

Certainly, my reasons for doing topic work had changed during the term from 'learning about a subject' to gaining skills which would enable the child to extract and present information on any subject. In assessing the degree of success in the term's work I have looked for evidence that the children have transferred skills introduced in one topic to another topic and have adapted them to their own way and use.

The following term, a student involved them in a topic on China. Positive moves were made to compare the two countries and their ways of living. The children were able to recall many of their impressions of France, and began to raise different types of questions — ones which were much harder to research and answer, but which required them to reflect and speculate.

Several terms have passed since I changed the emphasis and the transfer and extension of many skills is still becoming apparent. For example, as part of the 'France' topic, I had chosen the process of making champagne as a way of introducing the annotated diagram — numbered picture sequences with a short explanation. This has now become a common way of presenting not just processes, but life cycles of animals. An old method I know, but one which the children now select for themselves.

Alternative ways of extracting and presenting information have become common for many of the older children. However, the safe and easy 'writing and a picture' method is still favoured by those who are not confident and adept at finding information, organizing it to their own requirements and presenting it in a different way. The children still find that using several reference books to glean facts on a subject takes a little bit longer and requires more effort. Copying straight from the book is still the easiest way if they can get away with it. Nevertheless more of the children are prepared to put greater thought, depth and energies into their work. What I need now is another Methusulah or something equally stimulating!

Chapter 5:
Writing Processes in Topic Work

Elaine Gethins

This chapter reveals how a top junior class followed up a residential trip to Poole Harbour. Elaine Gethins used her experience of developing the writing processes to help the children to plan, draft, edit and above all to be aware of their audience.

This led the children to devise many interesting alternative ways of presenting their information and ideas with their audience during a class 'open day'. From their evaluation of their experiences the class clearly learnt many new and varied skills.

At the end of March my class of 10–11-year-old children spent a residential week in Poole. This was intended to provide starting points for topic work for most of the following term. The total topic work included maths investigations, art work, map making and language work.

For some time I had become dissatisfied with the quality of topic work previously undertaken with my class and to reflect on the reasons for this dissatisfaction, especially with how information books were being used. In addition, other questions had emerged, such as who should plan the topic work and how much should the teacher direct. So, during the Easter holidays, as I planned how we might tackle the follow-up work, my aims crystallized as:

1 Working alongside the children and for the work to be less teacher directed.

2 Enabling the children to take a more active role in the development of their topic work.
3 Allowing the children to have a choice in their area of study based on interest, but friends would also be able to work together.
4 Improving the children's information skills, the ways of collecting and recording data and the ways of interpreting and presenting the data.

Initially, the whole class jointly contributed to making a topic web of the main areas for investigation. The children each chose one area which interested them, for example, the harbour, fish, birds, shells, castles, buildings and plants. This procedure provided the basis for groups. I hoped that by this process of self-selection, the children would be better motivated, as it was they who had decided their own area for topic work.

Each group had their own brainstorming session and produced their own more detailed web. The groups then made a collection of available resources which mainly comprised books from the school and county libraries. They also used booklets collected on the trip.

General Approach to the Work

Getting Started

So often at this stage, children rush to books to 'find out all they can' about a topic. This can lead to paging through a book to find something relevant and then copying sections of text. As teachers we must help children learn to use reference books more purposefully and effectively. It is, therefore, important for the children to identify the questions they want to answer, before turning to a book or other resources. Specific questions also help them make better use of the index and contents page.

To try to encourage this more purposeful approach to using information books, each mini-group was asked to think of questions to which they wanted to find an answer. Some children found it difficult to think of suitable, sensible questions: some being too specific, such as, 'How many men can a Viking longboat carry?' and some being too general such as, 'What are Vikings like?' Both of these kinds of questions caused difficulties later when trying to locate the information. Obviously, there was a need for discussion about 'good' questions at this stage.

The next step was to collect together questions on the same theme. This helped to split up the work for individual children and helped them to make efficient use of the reference books. The idea of formulating questions and classifying questions was new at this time. While some children did this cheerfully, others needed persuading. At this stage I suspect the children adopted this practice because it was suggested rather than because the basic logic was understood. The children did improve at question-making during the term.

Although the members of the mini-groups were investigating different aspects of a topic, they were encouraged to work as a group, to help each other solve problems, to share the resources and to point out relevant information to each other. Most groups did cooperate but there were a few individuals who did not. Even though their motivation was high, some children found that they were unable to share the work. In one group of three girls, one girl pursued her own independent investigation, while another girl hoarded her questions and answers and was determined not to share them. This led me to realize the importance of the social skills needed for working together as a team. This, perhaps, needs to be a continuous focus at all ages.

As the children began to collect information, it was recommended that they use a grid or a chart. Questions were written along the vertical axis and resources on another axis. The boxes created by this grid format had another effect. There was only room for notes or key points. It was therefore impossible to copy sections of text. However, some children experienced difficulty in selecting main ideas and making intelligible notes. Hence, the charts proved an effective medium for collecting data neatly and concisely. More importantly, the data was organized in a form that the children could readily understand and use.

I wanted to work closely with the topic groups especially at the beginning stages. During the week there were four uninterrupted blocks of time when half the class was involved with topic work and the rest were engaged in individual work. An individual work check sheet was devised with certain tasks starred that had to be completed during the week and other options suggested for the remaining time. Generally the children liked the responsibility and choice in planning the order of their work. The system worked well but it was still difficult giving enough time to the topic groups. However, once the groups' objectives were clearly established, it became easier because the children knew the direction of their enquiries without continual consultation.

Throughout the project we had many class discussions concerning common problems such as using an index or contents page, reasons and strategies for grouping questions, and possible forms for the final presentation including expected qualities for an upper junior standard. The conclusions were put on 'help cards' and made available for reference in the classroom. Also, sharing the progress of various groups helped to make the 'process' public, so an understanding of this way of working was fostered. Once, we also discussed the problems created for me if children queued to ask questions or if they did not work sensibly. Some strategies evolved that helped the children be more independent. Generally the class discussion technique helped us progress through the project, sorting out problems along the way (see photographs 2, 3, 4).

Keeping the Work Going

Topic work often stops at this stage with a written presentation and perhaps a picture. I began to understand that there was little value in simply collecting facts. The next step was to evaluate the information and to look for patterns or connections that would lead to further thinking or speculation. This was a difficult stage for both the children and myself. However, as time went on, our confidence grew, and the occasions when we searched for reasons to explain a pattern or a puzzle proved to be the most exciting and rewarding.

The technique used most often was comparison. This enabled children to try to identify similarities and differences, and then to move on to cause and effect. For example, a boy studying fish compared their breathing to that of humans; medieval weapons were compared to modern day weapons; the birds group tried to identify features which differentiated between waders and divers from their data on observed birds. The plants group set up an experiment to compare bean seeds growing in salty water and plain water. It would have been interesting to repeat the experiment with seaweed but we did not have a sample. They also looked for a connection between the colour of the seaweed and the preferred depth of habitat.

Some groups explored attitudes toward particular facts. For instance, a boy studying smugglers, first researched background information about who the smugglers were, what they smuggled and why, and why the government was so against it. Then he sought the class' opinions about the justification for smuggling and their attitudes to the risks involved. Another boy, working on a pleasure boat design, used a questionnaire to help decide what features to include to make the boat popular. A girl studying medieval clothes focused on women's clothes and the comparison to present-day clothes led in turn to thinking about modern women who wear long dresses. She wrote to the multicultural advisor who brought saris into the classroom. Everyone had a chance to wear the saris and the real experience of comfort, materials and colours as well as the reasons for wearing them, helped us relate to similarities and differences with medieval dress.

This project also posed difficulties for me personally because I was learning the approach to the work with the children. There were times when I didn't really see where it was all leading. Certainly there was a need for support from colleagues in the classroom, working with groups and answering my questions and providing the guidance necessary to develop this work. Also, my knowledge of the writing process helped me see a pattern to this approach to topic work.

This was especially so in the early stages, when the questions were being formulated and sorted. I was worried as the work seemed to progress very slowly and there was less visual evidence of the work. However, the children needed this time in order to come to terms with the new responsibilities of planning their own work and to allow the quality of their ideas to develop.

Hence, we adopted a new policy of display. Instead of only displaying finished products, we also displayed work in progress which helped us to focus on the process itself and allow us to share common problems and successes. However, the school staff and parents needed to understand this aspect. So, when visiting children and adults came into the classroom, I took the opportunity to explain the stages of the work to the adults. One mum said that some of our topic discussions had also been debated at home. So it seems the children were engaged in active thinking about the way they were finding information and using it and enjoying it.

Topic Work as a Process of Learning

During this project, I began to see links between the approach to topic work described above, and the writing process based on Graves work, that was already becoming established in my classroom. Now, I realize, this general way of working can be applied to most areas of the curriculum. In essence it is about going deeper with one aspect of a study, rather than skimming the surface of a wider area. The chart compares the main stages for writing and topic work:

	Stages	Writing	Topic Work
1	Motivation purpose	Have a clear sense of audience and reason for writing from the start	By allowing children to define their topic and identifying what they want to find out
2a	Collecting impressions	Deciding on something to say based on a chosen topic or experience Brainstorm for ideas, words and phrases	Focus on an area for investigation Brainstorm for questions to answer about a topic
2b	Planning	Sorting ideas, does it make sense?	Sorting questions into groups of similar types to aid in sharing work
3	Drafting/ taking notes	Putting thoughts on paper	Using reference books, locating, extracting, recording information
4	Sharing responses	Getting and responding to opinions from other children Using discussion skills	Working as a group cooperatively Help to speculate solve problems

5	Editing and organizing	Are the ideas in the best order?	Looking for patterns and connections in the data
		Is the lead sentence captivating?	Interpreting, comparing and evaluating data
		Can anything be left out? etc.	Reorganizing and integrating data
6	Mechanics/ check		Grammar and spellings
7	Final copy		Decide on form Make a best effort of presentation for the audience
8	Present- ation/ celebration	Book, letter, song, label, poem, poster etc	As for writing but also tapes, models etc

The main parallels are:

1 *Motivation and purpose*: The child is made an active participant from the start by using his/her experience, ideas, interest and knowledge. This is in contrast to merely wanting to please the teacher rather than trust their own thinking. This problem, in the context of topic work is illustrated in the following extract:

> T: How is your list getting on? Can I see? You have rubbed it all out? Why did you do that?
> D: You didn't seem to like it.
> T: That's no reason to rub it out! What are you going to do now? ...
> T: What are you doing now, D?
> D: Writing it out again.
> T: You mean the one you just rubbed out?
> D: Yeah.
> T: Why?
> D: Dunno ... Well, you seemed to want it back again!

Having recently observed nursery school children working purposefully and independently, I began to wonder what happens to children's self-confidence during their school life. In many ways, without realizing it, we perhaps strip them of independence. For instance, we sometimes overlook the skills of thinking and manipulation that they already possess. It is sad to see older children remaining emotionally uninvolved with their work and simply aiming to please the teacher.

2   *Collecting and planning*: By brainstorming for ideas or questions, the child is developing the skills of planning and making decisions about the direction of his/her work. This stage can be messy and untidy but the main aim is to get something down on paper that can be worked on. Also, the skills used in sorting ideas or questions help children organize their work. Learning to look for common themes needs time and encouragement for it to become a natural way of working. However, there was initial reluctance to try a new way of working, as the following extract from the Viking group shows:

T: How are you getting on?
A: We've got these questions and now we've got to get the answers.
T: Can I see the questions?
L: We have to sort them first.
T: How are you going to do that?
L: Well, we see which ones go together.
T: Well which ones do you think go together?
A: There's these ones all about the boat, and then the others. And then we've got some about fighting.
T: And when you've sorted them, what do you do then?
A: Write them out again.
T: Can I make a suggestion?
L: Yeah.
T: If you get some scissors, you could cut each of these questions into separate bits of paper. Then you could sort them into piles. It might be easier than trying to sort them in your head. ... Then you could just stick them down without having to write them all out again.
L: I don't mind writing!

As teachers, we feel guilty about asking children to copy work too often, knowing it is a mindless activity. Do children accept copying as an easy option because it does not demand thinking? This can be a form of time wasting.

3   *Drafting ideas and taking notes*: Using the information books (locating, extracting, recording) was a vital stage. In terms of topic work the problem of reading and understanding some texts posed severe difficulties when trying to take notes that made sense. This problem was highlighted in the group studying sea birds. While struggling to sort out general features of waders and divers, they met vocabulary problems with words such as, gait, crustaceans, molluscs and marine invertebrate. Although the group worked very well together and most were able readers, they needed substantial support to overcome this hurdle. The actual format of notes posed a problem too, for, using sentences may have become an established safe way of writing, but taking notes is a useful skill that also needs to be taught. It is important to discuss the occasions and reasons for choosing a note form rather than a sentence form. This is evident in the following extract:

> *T*:   Can I see how you are writing it down? Oh, I see, you are doing sentences. Is this a page of notes, or is it the final page?
> *R*:   It's just notes.
> *T*:   Why do you do it all out in sentences? It must take a long time.
> *S*:   If it is just notes, you forget what they mean sometimes.
> *T*:   Hm ... That's true.
> *R*:   It's good as it takes up more time this way, too!

It seems that writing in sentences takes longer and demands less thinking than taking notes. Children can be reluctant to make the effort to develop this technique (see photographs 5, 6).

4   *Sharing*: Without doubt, the discussion skills take longest to develop. Children need to learn how to give constructive criticism, how to respond to it and to see the purpose of it. This stage needs a model with the teacher taking part for a time, to set the right tone. The children are learning to value their own opinions and that of their peers.

Many of our most useful discussions were based on problems with the process of this approach to topic work. When this way of working is more established, more reporting back time needs to be organized to give the children greater opportunity to express the content of their topic discoveries orally.

5   *Editing and organizing*: For me personally, the idea of improving a piece of writing is more familiar than the process of trying to discover

connections and patterns from factual material. Some examples of this have already been discussed in the sections above. At this stage speculation is important. Some children by 10 or 11 years have already learned to ignore their own ideas as in the fish group:

R: They lay their eggs in a lot of different places.
T: Oh yes ... I wonder why that is?
R: It could be so its safer. The crabs can't eat them if the eggs are in the sand.
S: The other fish wouldn't see them either, if they lay them in sea-weed. Look, this one's laying in an old sea-shell. That's safe.
R: The sea-weed could be camouflage.
T: That's a super lot of ideas.
S: Shall I put them down?
T: Yes, why not?
R: But it's not what the book says.
T: You could write down all the things that you think of and then see what the books say about it. You may have thought of lots of things that the books haven't thought of.
S: So I'll put it on a different page. What shall I call it?
T: Well, you could call it 'My ideas' perhaps. Well done, they were marvellous ideas. Good thinking.

Encouragement and praise are important to build up the child's confidence in his/her thinking. Throughout the sessions, the children were encouraged to give their own opinions if a question could not be answered using the reference books. This caused some problems in the presentation stage where children used their speculations as facts. Learning how to handle this was an important part of the learning experience.

6   *Checking*: The final stages of both writing and topic work are the same. The need for mechanical accuracy and quality of presentation are important to celebrate the work and share it with others.

7   *Presentation*: Difficulty arose when the children tried to present their information in certain formats. Turning facts into questions seemed to cause the most problems. More demands were made on the children because the facts were being used and not just restated as a piece of writing.

Apart from the social skills needed for working in groups, groups can experience difficulties in making collective decisions. After a long non-conclusive deliberation, the shells group were persuaded to make a chart to summarize the reasons for and against using different formats for presenting their information:

Ideas	Good Things	Bad Things
Folder	Lots of people can look	Gets messy and lost
Book	It keeps nice and looks good	Boring, just facts
		Only one person
		can look at a time
Tape	Saves writing	We need pictures
Chart	Easy	Boring/just look
Quiz cards	Nobody's done it, not babyish	Difficult to get the information
Choose Your Own Adventure	Good fun	Babyish

The group decided that the quiz card, Choose Your Own Adventure book or an ordinary book were the best. They quickly went round the class to find out which was the most popular. The result was the adventure book. Even so the children nearly reverted to making their own books because not all the group members were prepared to collaborate. These problems seldom arise with individual work. However, coming to terms with the skills of working together as a group is important preparation for the real world. Further issues are discussed in the following section.

Developing a Sense of Purpose and Audience in Topic Work

The topic stage that often does not match with the writing process is the initial stage: that of motivation or purpose for doing the work. Previously, I had planned the topic independently of the children. In the case of the Poole topic, the residential visit came first and then we were simply finding out more about different areas, in groups which were based on a common interest.

Motivation should have been high, but still some children seemed satisfied with a minimal effort for their work and much support and encouragement were needed to extend the initial response. A contributing factor was perhaps the lack of clear purpose at the beginning. It seems some children avoid personal involvement with their work so there is little pride. If work is believed to be 'for the teacher', have we taught the children to remain detached and promote an 'I don't care' attitude? Certainly attitudes influence the quality of work both positively and negatively. Teachers must take responsibility to address this problem.

In terms of developing manual, social and intellectual skills, topic work provides countless opportunities. But from the child's point of view, is the intended audience just the teacher? When writing, the child ought to have the purpose and audience clearly in mind from the start (ie a letter, shopping list, story for a friend, a recipe, a poster etc.). I began to realize that topic work also needs to be made more purposeful for the child to justify their effort of working at the process of thinking about information.

As the children began to select ways of communicating their information, I noticed that many of the pieces of work were intended to be used, read or looked at. It seemed natural to share these products with a wider audience. We decided that we would invite the five other classes in the school into our room to look more closely at the work. This purpose did help us in focusing the final stages of the topic work.

Now that I am more aware of the importance of purpose and audience, I will be tying to encourage this much earlier, preferably at the start of the topic. However, as work develops, it may be necessary to redirect or reconsider the audience. The key idea is to keep the purpose in mind.

In one class discussion we were thinking of the various forms in which topic work may be presented. Our discussion helped establish criteria for quality of different formats which proved a useful guide as the work was being completed. For example, a poster has little writing, but this actually makes it harder to decide what to include to convey a message accurately. Similarly, pictures have to be selected for the best effect.

The children tried to show their learning and their thinking in the final product. They tried to choose a format that suited their data and their interests. The variety was extensive including posters, models, surveys, reports, historical fiction, poems, quiz cards, a choose-your-own adventure type of book, plans, tapes and brochures.

I was surprised that some children had difficulty in actually handling the data and changing it into another form. In discussing the making of quiz cards, serious thought was given to what was a 'fair' question. For example, a closed Yes/No question or one requiring a specific point of information was thought unfair, as the reader either knew it or didn't. The children decided that a good question gave enough information in the writing or the picture for the user to make an educated guess at the answer. Also there should be enough information given or speculation offered for the user to learn something.

The Final Sharing of the Work

We used an assembly time to present the topic work to the school. The groups tried to explain the stages of their investigations including some of the problems, and they presented their final product as well. During the rest of that day, classes visited our classroom on a rota basis. The idea was to provide an opportunity for the various 'topic products' to be used.

For the visits, my children were spaced around the classroom with their work. One group with a tape to listen to used a small room across the corridor. The atmosphere was relaxed. The visiting children were encouraged in a casual way to spend time with different groups. It was very enlightening from my point of view to stand back and listen to the children explaining their work. Some children, not always the most able ones, used excellent natural skills to communicate their ideas orally in an effective way. The visiting children were from 5 years to 10 years, so a flexible delivery was also required. Circumstances made it necessary that all classes visited on the same day. It may have been more leisurely if perhaps we had spread the visiting over several days. Nevertheless, the day satisfied the need to use the topic products, and it gave my children a chance to share their work with the rest of the children and adults in the school (see photographs 15, 16).

Many occasions arose during the visits that made my children feel proud and that the effort had been worthwhile.

We followed the sharing day with an evaluation discussion which proved to be very worthwhile. During the discussion the children were honest with their criticism. We debated possible improvements and the main points raised will make specific areas to focus on the next time we share our work within the classroom or beyond. The exercise also revealed some of the problems, worries and attitudes of the children that otherwise I may not have noticed. Again this will help with our future planning and preparation as well as making me more sensitive to the children's feelings in similar situations.

The Assembly

In general, the children thought that an assembly should be presented in an active way to make it interesting for those watching and listening. They decided our particular assembly was good because there was not too much speaking. Also the audience had things to see and wonder about. The children thought that presenting their work or speaking in assemblies provided good opportunities for them to learn to express their ideas orally and to come to terms with nervousness.

However, some children thought the assembly was dull and that they could have explained their work more fully. Occasionally the audience was chatting which was distracting, perhaps they were bored? The children decided that asking questions was better than reading out passages because the audience is more involved. Probably more practice would have helped the children to speak up more and to include some expression in their voices. Some children felt frightened to speak, some left out parts because of nervousness, and occasionally one child said what another child had intended saying. We identified a need for notes to help give confidence. The skills involved making notes and using them for oral communication.

Sharing in the Classroom

Generally my children said they enjoyed having the visitors in the classroom and seeing their work used. We thought the children had enjoyed their visit which was confirmed by subsequent thank you letters. The children claimed to be less nervous in the classroom so they were able to explain their work properly. They also said they had tried to make the visit 'nice' — but there were some problems.

The whole experience of putting the children in the position of teachers was instructive. This was particularly true of some children who discovered the need to find ways of modifying and improving their presentation to suit different groups. One girl, who had a poster about fish, found that if she asked the children to find which fish they liked on the poster, it made them look carefully. This led on to conversation about fish as pets and so on. This was more interesting and active than children just glancing, reading and moving away. Obviously some groups with written pieces of work had to change their approach with young infants.

Sometimes the noise level was rather high in the classroom, especially when a tape recorder was being used. Some children found it harder to 'keep law and order'. They realized that it was annoying to be interrupted and to notice other children not listening. One particularly bossy girl was not too pleased when children drifted away before her session was finished. The same girl tended to dominate the presentation of her group's work, which upset the other group members. So many social lessons were learned when we shared our work with the school.

Final Evaluation

My initial aims were achieved and in addition my own understanding of topic work developed by thinking through the learning process. This way of working posed many problems, but these were outweighed by the genuine excitement that engulfed the class or groups with various particularly successful aspects of the work. Most children took pride and pleasure in explaining their work to the school.

My role was to enable the groups to take some responsibility and yet to guide them to question and think more deeply. My main regret was allowing so many different topic subjects. Although the children really did value the choice, the subjects were so diverse it was impossible to relate them to each other. To restrict the choice to two or three main areas would make the organization easier. Also I feel the quality of my support would increase with fewer groups. It is easy to be critical with hindsight. The important thing is to learn from the less successful elements and improve for the future.

Although I came to understand this approach to topic work as a process similar to the Graves writing process, this does not mean that all stages need to be rigorously followed for every topic. In fact since the Poole topic work, there has been another topic that generated most excitement by finding and using a very wide range of resources. In this case, discovering where to find evidence was the valuable part of helping the children learn about learning.

Being aware of the process for both writing and topic work has helped me to understand the possible stages of development of pieces of work. Thinking of the process has helped me to focus on the most important aspects:

— the initial purpose of the work;
— developing a questioning and enquiring attitude;
— sharing ideas with others during the development stages and also the final presentation.

I have learned to allow time for progression, rather than rushing the children to the product stage. When the children are active and in control of their learning, their independence and self-confidence are increased. All that is required is that the teacher is conscious of the possibilities and is prepared to step back to allow the children to use their own ideas. The teacher's role needs to be one of an enabler/guide as well as a teacher/helper, but not a dictator/director.

Chapter 6:
Topic as a Way of Working

John Barrett

The next chapter, shows a rather different approach to topic work. In this case-study children pursue their own interests, individually or in pairs, for the major portion of each school day.

The chapter articulates the philosophy of one particular school and demonstrates how it works in practice. Here, topic work takes up almost the entire curriculum and the children's progress is monitored by the children themselves in conjunction with the teachers.

The topic work described in this chapter is not offered as a definitive statement. It simply represents a stage in one school's understanding of it. The model is not one that has first been constructed and then applied but one that has been and continues to be abstracted from shared experience.

Topic Work and the Curriculum

In the simplest possible terms our job is about bringing children to understand, to appreciate and to enjoy the world in which they live and their own unique relationship with it. The origin of the word 'educate' translates simply 'to lead out'. Such a purpose should be reflected in all the school's planning.

Life and learning are inextricably bound together. Schools can unwittingly institutionalize learning. The choice of content, the manner of its implementation and the context in which it is seen can so readily serve to disassociate the learning process from personal daily experience. What messages do children take away from school about learning from their experience of it? The question is critical to the perception children develop of the purpose of learning, their appetite for it and their competence in it. The insistent objective must be to develop willing, competent and autonomous learners who are interested and questioning of what goes on in their world.

It is as a natural consequence of these comments that topic work, if it is to be the means of developing such skills, should take up a principal curriculum position. Like so many educational terms it is one that is variously interpreted. It is understood here to mean such work as arises from some personal experience and provides the focus for sustained study. It does not rule out the use of secondary sources but is founded in the belief that children of primary school age need the support of recent experience to enable their reflections, comments and explorations to have integrity. Such secondary sources as are used must play a largely supportive role rather than a leading one. There must be a breadth and depth of personal experience alongside which, in due course, second-hand material can be used.

Whatever the educational purpose that is established it must be supported by a curriculum structure that can reflect its intention and be implemented in a manner that is sympathetic to children's natural learning characteristics. These two factors must now be developed.

Topic Work and the Child

The primary child's interaction with his world comprises countless experiences: some small-scale and fleeting; others more sustained. It is through these experiences that a child builds up a picture of his world and his relationship with it. The teacher's task must be to engineer the circumstances that promote a broad range of experiences and create the opportunity to explore and reflect on them in a variety of ways. The cumulative effect is to add to the child's understanding, enjoyment and appreciation of his world and the possibilities that it presents. There is, in the course of the experience and the reflection on it, a fusion of self and experience. As the number and range of their experiences extend so new understanding is added to old; so patterns emerge and new possibilities present themselves.

Producing work of quality requires effort and increasingly sustained effort. Such effort is the consequence of commitment; a commitment that can only arise when the child is interested. Barnes (1975) commented that,

> to become meaningful a curriculum has to be enacted by pupils as well as by teachers. By enact I mean come together in meaningful communication, talk, write, read books, collaborate, become angry, learn what to do and say. (p. 14)

Children will do a great deal for their teachers because they like them and would wish to please them but this, of itself, is an inadequate basis for enactment.

Children are more capable of sustained attention when they are committed imaginatively to the subject in hand; when it fits into what they see as worth getting to grips with. For, as Barnes says,

> When the boundary between school knowledge and action knowledge is low and easy to cross, we can expect the pupils to be able to take an active part in the formulation of knowledge. (*ibid*, p. 30).

Too often the subject matter is centred on what the teacher knows while the reality of the child's experiences are excluded.

What must be aimed for is a shared and therefore mutually supportive experience; joint exploration in which children are not directed by a need to determine what it is the teacher might wish them to say (what Rosen describes as 'empty verbalism') but in which children and teachers exchange the products of their own thinking. The children get a sense that the things around them are significant — are worth paying close attention to and thinking deeply about. There is an infectious quality to the work that involves some form of personal investment.

This sort of commitment is strengthened when children feel they have a stake in the task, when they have helped shape it and explored its possibilities; when in fact they own their own purposes.

The need for satisfaction and a sense of fulfilment are important ingredients especially when the going gets tough. In work that offers children a genuine purpose when there is a 'for real' quality about it then satisfaction is a built-in component and fulfilment a more likely outcome. Children do not live at a 'once-removed' level from their world. They are 'doors' learning through what they themselves do, not what the teachers do. The teachers cannot give children the product of their learning; they create the climate, the environment and help them develop the skills, but it is their own experience they should be examining and the exchange of their own thinking. They should be making and using their own knowledge and becoming for that moment authoritative, experts on their topic theme and so developing a trust and confidence in their own perceptions, ideas and feelings.

Aspects of the Curriculum

There are two important levels of curriculum understanding. There is that level that we engage in to deepen, refine and enrich our understanding. We focus perhaps on some strand of the curriculum to identify and expose the possibilities it possesses, or more minutely on some detail to ensure uniformity of vocabulary and approach. It seems rather like a car manual; the document to refer to in relation to specific queries until experience replaces the need for reference.

The other level of curriculum understanding might best be described as the 'mind's eye' curriculum. This represents the essential framework in which all the many strands and details alluded to above have a part. It must become familiar enough to inform the thinking of teachers at every teaching moment. It is because of the sheer complexity of the task, because of the unitary nature of children's experience and because no teacher can work in isolation mindless of what went before or should come after, that it is such an essential understanding to maintain. Teachers make countless on-the-spot decisions during any one day. There needs to be a rationale that guides those decisions. Thus armed teachers are more able to respond to the needs of the moment, confident that their responses serve both the current needs whilst at the same time contributing to the broad and long-term objectives of the school. The greater the involvement of the staff in identifying those two levels of understanding the more effectively they will be carried into the classroom.

It is necessary to give the broad outline of this second level of curriculum understanding. It seeks simply to identify the principal strands, the role they play and how they relate to each other.

There are three curriculum strands:

There is the subject matter itself. This refers to the aspect of the children's world that they are studying and falls into three broad 'areas of knowing'.

(i) *The Physical World*: This encompasses the exploration of the earth's materials, living things; it involves exploring notions of change and the physical environment itself.

(ii) *The Human World*: The humanities have man as the centre of their concern; man in relation to his community and environment. In the primary phase this concentrates very much on the child's community and near-at-hand environment but as his understanding and imaginative capacities grow it paves the way to consider them in other times and places.

(iii) *The Spiritual World*: Experience in this sphere falls into two broad types. There is that in which, through experience and reflection, we consider our own position in the world and how we think and feel about that world. There is also the exploration of others' religions, celebrations, festivals and symbols.

The second principal strand is concerned with the skills of knowing. These provide the means of exploring and making sense of the learning experience and of taking it on into further dimensions. Skills are the tools of life. They are as such subservient to a given purpose and where possible their introduction and development should arise and grow within the context of a clear purpose; the need creating the demand. The effort that anyone will bring to the mastering of a new skill will very largely be determined by the purpose they see for it. The increasing depth and range of children's experience will in turn call for an increasing range of and facility in these skills. They have been described as the 'amplifiers of human capacitors'. There are clearly key skills that cut across all learning and there are those that relate more particularly to one 'area of knowing'. It is important to identify them in both levels of curriculum understanding. At the simplest level they seem to fall into two broad categories: the expressive skills and the interpretive skills.

The third curriculum strand is really an extension of the skills of knowing but is separately identified to support the achievement of breadth and balance. It is concerned with the modes of knowing; that is with the nature of the response to any experience. Children's responses whether spontaneous or reflective are to a large extent emotive, personal and egocentric. They can also be 'matter of fact' or conversely playful and imaginative. These modes are not exclusive of each other. Increasingly, as children develop it is important to determine which is to be the dominant mode. Are they being scientists or poets, historians or inventors. This is clearly necessary in order to help the teacher to support the child in saying what he has to say, in making sense of his sense and doing so most appropriately to his purpose.

A clear and shared understanding of such a curriculum framework in its simplest forms is a prerequisite to the capacity for handling such a complex task. If teachers are to solve the problem of breadth and progression and to match children's ability and interest then, the curriculum must be reduced to manageable proportions, to a form that can be translated into Monday morning.

Practical Considerations

The first practical consideration is the time-scale involved. This relates primarily to the child's maturity. In the early days of this junior school topics tend to comprise perhaps only three or four pieces of work over two or three days. The time-scale relates to the capacity of the child to maintain interest. Small scale experiences simply explored add to the child's understanding of his world at the same time as seeds are being sown about how to plan and present work in a variety of ways as new skills are introduced so that increasingly the child can more genuinely engage in the exercise of choice of medium and mode of comment.

Progressively the child becomes capable of sustained effort. This topic is not the subject matter for each Thursday afternoon but may be the focus of attention for continuous periods, a day and a half at a time, as the level of interest and the discipline of the material being worked on may dictate. At other times alternative activities will take precedence and for the time being that topic is put to one side.

The second consideration is choice. The exercise of choice is an important life skill and children need experience both in the making of choice and the consequences of doing so. There will be times when children determine the topic itself and as they extend the range of their skills they can increasingly select what they believe to be most appropriate to the task in hand.

An important objective is to encourage children in the belief that the things that interest them and the things they see and do are significant and worthy of study. To take what they bring and enlarge the experience for them is an important means of achieving this belief. There need, however, to be controlling factors. The school itself exercises control in the choice of starting points it introduces into the school and its grounds. Children also want to know that while their ideas will not be coldly rejected they will need to relate to some artifact or recent experience.

A further consideration is group size. Most topics are undertaken in groups of two to four children. This proves to be largely a self-governing consideration, less of a conscious objective than a consequence of the wish to use topic themes that accommodate children's perspectives of their world; that heightens the significance of their own experiences; that allows them to explore small-scale first-hand experiences from all sorts of view points and to emerge from such studies with knowledge and experience that in that moment was not shared by others.

This is not to undermine the value of the class or even the school topic. There will be occasions when perhaps a half-class (a minibus load) may go to the market for the morning or the whole class will go on a fungi forage or search the stream. Such themes tend to be shorter ones. It is harder to sustain genuine commitment by each child or to involve them in the detailed planning of all the possibilities in a larger group. About once or twice a year the whole school will start for a week a theme such as 'an inventors' week' or 'an authors' week' or the planning of their own fete in which they assume responsibility for the running of the whole afternoon. This was undertaken to support the education of a child in India which became part of a comparative study for some older children. Of practical necessity the school itself must be able to resource and facilitate 'for real' learning. It needs collections of 'things' as well as books. The school grounds too need developing and the near at hand environment should be exploited to the full. Children should be able to comment in detail about the environment and community in which they live. In turn residential trips offer the opportunity to extend what has been locally undertaken. Teachers have to become skilled exponents in creating and exploiting learning opportunities.

Further, it is important to develop in the children, from the beginning, an increasing facility in the handling and presentation of their work in a variety of ways. It is proper that they should share in that responsibility but it is also expedient in terms of teacher time.

Finally, an essential ingredient in a developing process is, of course, the evaluation of work undertaken. This occurs naturally at every stage where choices have to be made. However, it also needs to be formalized in some way at the completion of the topic. Records of such evaluations need to be brief and the work itself kept to provide examples of achievements to supplement the records.

The children should share in this process of evaluation for it sharpens their awareness of their own learning, of their strengths and weaknesses.

The format of these records should facilitate easy interpretation by other teachers. This can be achieved through a short paragraph following on from previous records to indicate the main developments. Such a paragraph should be shaped by the school's agreed analytic framework of objectives. This offers easy assimilation and yet allows the teacher the opportunity to capture the feel and character of the work, which a formal document can inhibit.

The manner of sharing this task will depend on the maturity of the child. It might take the form of a discussion about the work achieved and negotiation concerning the direction of future work. It is important that the evaluation should be a partnership so that the child grows in understanding and responsibility for their work.

A Chosen Topic

This final section will focus on one topic. The topic was not chosen for any merits it might have but simply on the grounds that it was one that was about to start, so its development could be more closely observed.

The Aviary: Ian and Mark (10-year-olds)

The topic choice was made by the boys. They had earlier in the term been on a residential trip and were engaged in a considerable amount of follow-up work. This provided a period for the idea to lie dormant; a period that the teacher used to test the commitment of the boys to this study — for Mark was a very impulsive child. In the event their enthusiasm survived the interval.

Teachers are subject to considerable pressures. This induces a sense of anxiety which often expresses itself in 'hurry' and, in that state of mind, the temptation is to by-pass the moments of struggle in which the learning moves forward and in effect 'to do' the learning for the pupils. An important purpose on the part of the teacher in this topic was to help the boys into a more participatory role.

The initial discussion between teacher and boys lasted a little over twenty minutes. That this dialogue was able to continue during the school day for a sustained period, with only one interruption, reflects the pattern of the classroom organization. Implicit is the principle that dialogue is important; that both social relationships and knowledge take form in the course of communication. The boys are learning what is expected of them and how they are expected to take part. There is a reciprocal relationship between teacher and pupils. Children will take part in dialogue to the degree that they believe their contribution is valued. The opportunity for sustained dialogue is the warrant for that belief.

The teacher's role had been to help shape, in practical terms, the ideas that were only half-formed in the boy's minds; to enable them to see their ideas in a way that might prove more productive to them. At the same time the teacher was setting an example of how things may be discussed. The acceptance of their contributions reinforced their own credibility in the boys' eyes.

In reviewing a taped recording of the discussion the teacher had asked forty-nine questions which fell into the following categories:

Questions requesting elaboration.
Questions seeking clarification.
Questions to maintain and support the idea.
Questions that invited confirmation of what had been said.

Following the discussion, the boys were sent off to explore and set down their ideas. The importance of discovering, together, for ourselves is expressed by Barnes (1979)

Our ability to make meaning is first developed in collaboration with others and gradually becomes an individual ability to think, feel and value for oneself. (p 59)

In this instance the teacher was hoping that Ian might exert pressure by questioning and insisting on rational answers and so help Mark to new levels of explicitness. They produced the following plan.

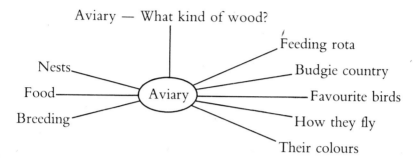

Aviary — What kind of wood?

These suggestions were discussed and the following refinements negotiated.

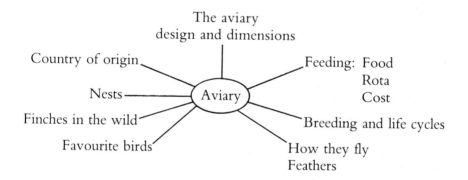

The aviary design and dimensions

The boys began work on their topic. It was completed some six weeks later. It comprised pieces of work most of which were included in a book. Nearly all written pieces began in note form and were worked on over two and sometimes three drafts. Drawings, paintings and models were developed from annotated sketches.

In reviewing the topic the work is set against the framework described earlier to judge both its contribution towards fulfilling those curriculum outlines and to help make sensible decisions about what may follow.

What follows is not a detailed analysis but simply what broad contribution was made.

Contribution of the Chosen Topic

(i) *Areas of knowing*

The topic lay principally in the category of the physical world and particularly with 'living things'. In that context the following areas were seriously studied.

The life cycle of birds with particular attention to birth and death. (The birds in the aviary bred successfully.)

The physical needs of birds: nests, climate and food.

Bird flight.

Definition of wild and non-wild creatures.

The heightening of respect for living things and the significance of our responsibility for the creatures of our world contributed to both the human and spiritual areas of knowing.

(ii) *Skills of knowing*

There are certain skills that will be exercised in every topic; there will be some that the topic in hand will particularly offer opportunity for development. In this topic the teacher was principally concerned with: skills of planning, the extension of the range of writing styles, the scientific skills associated with the study of living things.

(iii) *Modes of knowing*

In this topic most of the work was concerned with what might be described as the 'public mode'; that is with a variety of forms of expression (prose, questionnaires, models, drawings, interviewing, measurement, experimentation) but all expressed in a manner seeking maximum shared understanding. A few pieces were concerned with personal perspectives in which the intention lay with the articulation of feeling. (poetry, prose, painting.)

This topic is not offered as a highly successful example. There are undoubtedly aspects of it that could have been further developed or better exploited. It simply represents the best efforts of a teacher and two boys at a given time to fulfil those purposes outlined above.

Finally, it is important to say that the approach to topic work that this chapter describes, developed in relation to certain principles to which a group of teachers attached importance and took its form as a consequence of shared experience and reflection. The intention was to satisfy curriculum responsibilities in a manner that was hospitable to children of primary school age and that promoted the foundation of a productive attitude to life and learning.

Chapter 7:
Fostering Inventiveness With Young Children

Robert Hayes

Chapter 7 analyzes an exciting problem-solving approach to topic work. In common with many of the other case studies the children are given the responsibility for developing, presenting and evaluating their ideas. In contrast with the other case studies, in 'Fostering inventiveness with young children' the emphasis is not on information-seeking and gathering, but on employing the everyday experiences and scientific knowledge which the children have already accumulated. In this way children become information-users, in an inventive and imaginative fashion.

Is there a young Einstein in your class? How would you recognize a budding Einstein? What would you do with such a pupil? Do any of your practices prevent a budding Einstein from budding? How about a class full of potential Einsteins? What makes you think you haven't got such a class? Perhaps you already have!

The starting point for my investigation was a need to assist young children to move from being information-gatherers to information-users. At the time I had a very able class of 7–8-year-olds. They were knowledgeable and keen to learn, and I had great expectations for projects, topics and individual investigations taking off in many directions. But as the year progressed, although they worked hard and gave of their best in what ever was asked of them, many of the lines of thought and possibilities offered were not taken up to any great extent, and I was somewhat disappointed by this. I came to realize I had a class of knowledge-collectors busy filing facts in their memories, who did not think that information was for using, and did not think that their own ideas were important, valuable or worth developing. So the starting point for the project was to devise a way to make fact-gatherers into information-users.

Inventors are often highly original information-users. Many scientific breakthroughs and inventions were discovered by accident with a person noticing an unusual phenomena or effect, developing and using it, when others may not have noticed, or just commented and passed on. Vulcanized rubber, gramophone records, an anaesthetic, electric motors, radar, inoculation, fluorescent lights, and an antibiotic, are a few examples. Even Einstein didn't discover new evidence, he just devised an alternative theory and came to different conclusions to explain evidence that had already been available for fifty years. Hence, I wanted to create the same openness towards phenomena in the classroom situation in the hopes that this would encourage any potential Einsteins to 'bud'.

This chapter outlines the project; considers what was achieved; the difficulties for the teacher; implications for, and effects on, classroom practice; and how far this style of approach can be incorporated in the classroom. Fifty detailed recorded one-to-one discussions of the ideas the children came up with were made, and of necessity, much has to be omitted here, but I hope in the summaries to give some idea of the variety and flavour of outcomes. Some aspects are followed up in greater detail later.

The Progress of the Project

I noticed that in the classroom lessons went well on a topic on 'flying' where I had imagined and acted out the birth of the idea for hot air balloons by being Montgolfier sitting in his armchair casually watching the smoke go up the chimney and then suddenly realizing the possibilities. It also excited possibilities in children's minds. To us, of course, it now seems obvious, but to Montgolfier came the realization that whilst everything in the world falls down, smoke appears to fall up! He then thought that if he could catch hold of that smoke, he could go up as well! But how to catch hold of the smoke? Out he came with inverted paper bags, getting larger and larger until the idea worked. Children were surprised at how simple it was, and felt they could have easily done that — if only they had thought of it!

I decided to use this 'birth of an idea' approach, and present to the class four stimulus 'phenomena':

1   How a man on trying to mend and use his upright vacuum cleaner put the fan in back to front so that the air blew out. He noticed that friction was reduced and it slid easily across the carpet. (This has links with the idea of the hovercraft.)

2   How a bat emits a high pitched sound and listens for the echoes to detect prey and obstacles. (Links with sonar and echo sounders.)

3   How a man trying to develop a kind of electronic device noticed peculiar images on photographic film stored in a cupboard in the same room. Eventually it was tracked down as due to his device (and not faulty film), and the images were of the insides of whatever happened to be in front of the film in the cupboard. (Links with the discovery of X-rays.)

4   How a pond skater sits on the edge of a pond, with one foot on the water as a sensor. It can detect vibrations from any insect falling in and struggling and then home in on it for food. (No known links, the nearest idea is that of a seismograph.)

I introduced the idea of the lessons by using the way Montgolfier thought of hot air balloons as an example of seeing something interesting and using it for a great invention, explained that each of the ideas I was presenting could suggest many trains of thought that may lead to some other interesting inventions. There was no one 'right answer', pupils could suggest anything and everything they liked.

In the early stages, encouragement was especially necessary, and children kept coming up to ask 'Is this alright?' Without looking at the idea, I just reminded them that if they could explain it to me satisfactorily in their terms then it was automatically 'alright' and if they could work it out in greater detail it may turn out to be 'brilliant'.

First of all, to give some idea of the sorts of things that were suggested and what came up in discussion, a summary of the first session's main outcomes is given: from the vacuum cleaner blowing air out and the consequent reduction in friction, came five main sorts of idea, though, strangely, none were for hovercraft even though this had been popular in the pilot study.

1   The most popular idea was to use the air stream now being ejected by the cleaner as a source for propulsion. Ideas for 'turbo cars',

plane propulsion, helping hot air balloons, helicopters, jets, bikes and cars, and even propelling roller skates and a self-propelled vacuum cleaner. Discussion included points about how air was ejected in their inventions, how propellers worked, how to control speed and direction, what 'turbo' meant to children and what it meant in reality, about space travel, achieving balance of thrust with twin/multiple jets, computer controls, remote control, possible faults, and in one idea, the reversing of thrust to become a kind of air brake. Many of these ideas used the jet principle correctly and have many similarities with jets, rockets, propellers on planes and hovercraft, turbo engines, retro-rockets, and the experimental strap-on rocket back-pack, and the original flying bedstead.

2   Some children saw potential in the air stream being ejected to blow away, keep away or deflect objects, and used this for an idea for self-defence when under threat of attack. This may sound rather way out, but there is already an anti-mugging device based on an aerosol can; aerosol repellents for insects; dentists use compressed air to blow away particles in cavities in teeth before filling; and much research goes into ways of deflecting missiles off target. Who knows where some starting ideas may end up?

3   Some children realized that if the air was now blowing out of the vacuum cleaner, then all the dust in the bag would come out too, and used this for an idea for automatic emptying of the cleaner. Two children took this further, and realized that the bag could be filled with some material that it would be useful to have ejected in this way, and produced, in effect an electric wall paper paste spreader, and an electric seed planter. Discussion included control mechanisms to regulate flow, avoiding damage to the paper, and possible faults. For the seed planter, the bag contained seed, and discussion was around regulating the speed of ejection such that the seed would be propelled sufficiently fast to penetrate the ground but not so fast that it was crushed. Development included expanding this idea to carpet cleaning, floor washing, cement laying on motorways, laying liquid glass, watering plants or crop sprayers, and spraying floor polish. The principle behind the idea is well used in real life, most notably for spray painting of cars; but also is the principle behind all aerosols, many fire extinguishers, air compressors and equipment, cavity wall insulation injection, and

the reversible principle is well used in all self-fill/self-empty machines such as washing machines.

4   Two children recalling personal experiences of vacuum cleaners and the wires getting all tangled up and unplugging as you go from room to room, thought cordless cleaners would be a good idea. They described how easy it would be to use, and how it could be 'filled up with electricity', with a 'full up' indicator. This revealed much about their understanding of the nature of electricity and how vacuum cleaners worked — 'sucking in dust with the electricity'. The more I think about it, the more I am surprised that such an idea hasn't yet been marketed. There are rechargeable lawn mowers, power tools, shavers, torches, and rechargeable batteries for fitting to conventional electrical equipment.

5   One child decided on an unusual toy. The air coming out of the cleaner reminded him of a gun, but conventional cleaners suck in, so he devised a suction gun toy. It could be aimed at bits of dust by the child, the trigger pressed and the dust sucked up. There was the added advantage of serving a dual purpose, the child would have fun 'playing', and the parent would be pleased and praise the child on finding the house cleaned in the process! The idea got developed further for more practical purposes such as snow clearance. The principle of making play things/games for children from adults work or boring learning tasks is the basis of many toys, and the suck in/blow out principle used in dredgers, drain cleaners, pumps, bulk grain cargo handling, etc.

It has to be remembered that all these ideas and discussions were with children aged between 7 and 8-years-old! Much of the value to the children is seen within the context of the work described being the first tentative steps in a long continuous process that could lead to important and valuable outcomes in the future. If young children of 7-years-old can do all this, what would they be capable of at 18 or 21 years, if this approach were continued?

Benefits for the Children

First of all there needs to be an appreciation of the links that can be made between the children's ideas and current or future technology.

Secondly, when these processes are examined in greater detail it is possible to identify many other benefits ranging from re-evaluation of existing knowledge and its improved integration, to attitudes and strategies for dealing with strange and new situations.

Thirdly, after the presentation of the topic, the children were told to think of some use that could be made of the information given. They were left to decide for themselves how they wished to use the information and what they saw as 'useful'. In effect, the children were encouraged to be self-evaluative.

For some, the lessons and follow-up brought about a greater awareness that inventions don't just happen, or aren't that easily made. There is a need for a lot of preparatory work, careful analysis, assembling, altering, testing, development and reflection attached to designing some invention or achieving some aim. As ideas and proposals were continually modified, developed, altered or expanded, the children moved to a greater awareness of the concept of continuous development, a realization that many things are in a 'stage' of development, and that things are not fixed as they presently exist for all time. This has parallels with the concept of the construction of knowledge and the dynamic nature of knowledge.

There was also an awareness that when they got stuck they had reached a state of needing and being ready for an input of new knowledge, or more advanced ideas. This involved the children in a reflection on the sort of information required, active seeking of appropriate sources and the searching out of the specific information needed. Ultimately this can lead to the pure research approach where the knowledge needed is not available in any source, and the enquirer has to design and set up his own experiments to find out for himself the information he needs.

Further, as the sessions proceeded and confidence grew, children also came to realize that however strange and unusual topics may be, even at this young age, they do have a vast fund of knowledge and experiences that can be usefully brought to bear and can have many ideas and relevant thoughts.

Perhaps this confidence and pleasure with its consequent motivation engendered is one of the most valuable aspects of this approach. By their enthusiasm for their ideas, it seemed obvious that many thought that they really had done something good, something really worth achieving. Many wanted to continue improving their ideas, make alterations, continue development, etc, in their spare time, with me at lunch breaks, or a 'quick consultation' when I was on playground duty! Other children looked eagerly forward to future lessons, or wanted to know in advance what I was going to present.

A small note here that might be a pointer to something, is a feeling I had that this approach which mixes imagination with science is a good opener for and a way of getting girls involved in science. They enjoyed it just as much, if not more. Some girls, who I perceived as average, and who thought themselves as average generally and unlikely to take to this sort of topic, found themselves coming up with the most interesting, original and diverse ideas and in fact were rather good at it; whereas many boys' ideas were related solely to rockets, planes and military uses.

Anyhow, it could be that the most valuable aspect of all for the children was that by this different approach, instead of triggering off the more usual artistic creativity or creative story writing, it was a successful way to stimulate pupils' technological creativity. This may never have happened to them before, and may have opened up new horizons for them. It was an experience for me to see how 'alive' pupils became, and involved in their ideas, and how enthusiastically they communicated.

Teacher Responses

Each of the topics I was presenting could suggest many ideas and trains of thought: there was no one 'right answer'. This has implications for the way it is necessary to respond to the ideas. First of all I had to convince the children I really was interested in their ideas and really wanted to know, and the children had to be convinced that they could be original, self-evaluative, propose an idea and have their justification accepted. This meant that as well as giving continual encouragement, many times I had to accept what pupils said and not challenge it or query it. In this way children remained sure of my good intentions and weren't threatened by every little thing they said being picked up. When the relationship is firmly established the child can test ideas and decisions against the teacher, whose comments will focus the child's attention to areas that need development or spur thoughts in new ways.

I had to recognize and permit the expression of pleasure and pride in ideas as presented before moving on to how the idea could be developed. It was obvious that pupils were pleased with their ideas and achievements. In fact I felt I detected from some children some resistance to the desire on my part to encourage development of ideas, on the ground that they had already reached a very satisfactory level of achievement in just coming up with ideas of their own. It seemed as if they wanted to enjoy this good feeling for a while and not go rushing on. Even when I had heard similar ideas from other children, or knew of similar ideas in real life, I had to respond to each child individually and appreciate their contribution. To the child, who knows so much less about the world, his ideas can be to him, genuinely original and creative, and accompanied by great pleasure and excitement.

Sometimes in trying to explain their ideas children are lost for words, and one has to consider offering them some kind of vocabulary that can focus attention on subtle differences between the meanings of words and the meanings that the children are trying to convey.

Occasionally children can get stuck, or find it difficult to get started, in which case a teacher suggestion can help. But it is easy for children to just agree with the teacher, or the teacher to channel thoughts along teacher lines, so it is important to think of alternatives so the child is able to choose and make his own decision.

Expansion of the idea to other uses, and generalizing of the principle behind situation specific ideas were two intentions for discussion. But how to get children to think of alternatives or generalize without channelling their thoughts or telling them ideas?

Gains for the Teacher

I consider there are both professional gains and personal gains for the teacher from aspects of this approach. First of all, in seeing ways of being a better teacher, there are two types of benefit — seeing what children can be capable of, and learning about how children think. There are implications here for all areas of teaching as well, not just science.

In my discussions about the children's ideas, the wide range of topics which came up and about which young children can have significant thoughts, has caused me to reflect carefully and revise what topics should be rejected for classroom use as being too hard or obscure for young children to have anything to usefully contribute.

Secondly, the misunderstandings revealed in discussion show the nature of children's thinking, and the sorts of connections they are making. These also provide valuable leads into further development. For instance, I was surprised how many children seemed to think of sound as small solid particles. Echoes were these little particles bouncing back. This provides opportunities for the teacher to devise experiences and to help the child in ways appropriate to the child's level of thinking at the time.

Also important is a realization of the children's great openness to all aspects of any given situation; how they take note of all aspects of a situation without attributing degrees of significance to the elements, for which as yet they have little basis for judgment. It gives a chance to discover what children see as relevant, important or interesting when unaffected by adult values.

Not only this, it also reveals how pupils can connect these aspects to most unusual, and to us strange, parts of their own experience.

There are also personal benefits to the teacher. The children's ideas stimulated many trains of thought in my own mind, and stimulated my imagination, interest, and curiosity. I found I had taken for granted many things that occur with little appreciation of their incredible complications, or how much work must have gone into their development. I spent a lot of time wondering about things that I had never previously considered. Also, my thoughts went on from the children's other ideas, to thinking about just how I would try to solve some of the technical problems posed by their proposals, so that in effect, as well as seeing how far the children could go with their ideas, I also began to think how far could I go with their ideas as well! In the case of such ideas as the electric seed planter, paste spreader, and cordless vacuum cleaner, I wondered if they could become a reality and was full of admiration for their inventors! I felt that along with the children, I was discovering my own scientific creativity!

Difficulties in Building on Originality

The main difficulties for the teacher centre round understanding the children's logic and frame of reference and suspending the teacher's frame of reference and derived judgments; and around helping children to develop their ideas in their way without channelling their thoughts and taking over from them.

First of all it is very hard to suspend judgment about the value of the ideas. Also there is the question of following leads, particularly where many leads are offered or recognized from the children's idea. The question of deciding which of many leads I should follow, reveals that I may subtly channel the children. And finally, one of the most common and difficult problems to occur in developing pupils' ideas was that of making decisions about when to stop following the lead in order to supply some external information or ideas.

Overall, therefore, I felt that to tell the children my ideas or supply new information could be more distracting than helpful at this stage. I felt that the children needed to explore their own ideas more thoroughly, gain practice in extending them in their own ways, and have more confidence in themselves and the processes, before really being ready for, and able to appreciate much additional information or new ideas. In the long term, over a much greater period, I could envisage wonderful opportunities for extending thinking, and who knows — a classfull of Einsteins?

Back in the Classroom

Back in school, three years on, with a large full-time class of 6–8-year-olds, how has this approach changed my classroom practice? Well, I have made significant and far reaching changes in my classroom strategies, but of course, with all the will in the world, it is quite impossible to value, investigate, promote and follow-up every idea that children have in the ordinary classroom situation with large classes. Neither can that be expected of teachers.

However, that being said, I have decided since this investigation, that it is important and valuable to be more open to, and take up significantly more of, the children's ideas. I had thought I was fairly open, flexible, and encouraging, but now consider it is well worth the effort to be more so and I set out to try. How open, accepting, encouraging, one can afford to be, and the pace of change, is a matter for each individual to try out and work through. As things develop in the ways hoped for, one's ability to cater and respond to different situations and demands improves, one can be a bit bolder and more adventurous. For me, now, it is well established as a class norm that ideas are wanted and a standard part of my expectations. And every now and again, as time permits, I do my 'expectations of Einstein — this might be the idea of the century' response to a suggestion. The whole class takes it up and considers, reflects and contributes in all ways imaginable to see how far the idea can be taken: from detailed and acute observation of the practical set up to discover possible clues and leads with great interest and concentration, to rapid reference to other sources of information, and comparing similar situations, to name a few. This may be done over one or two afternoons, or extended over a longer period with the class coming back to it at intervals.

I have found a number of different strategies which can often encourage children to reveal their thoughts and theories. Asking for and challenging explanations of the commonplace, taken for granted, everyday events is one. Recently I asked children to explain how sunlight gets through the window glass, when we cannot. One child suggested that perhaps glass had very tiny holes in it, and this caused everyone to look very closely at the windows, and get magnifying glasses and the microscope out to help.

The second is to consider ways of achieving what seems impossible. In a recent topic on houses, it was agreed that usually the roof is put on last, so, what ideas did the children have for enabling the roof to be built first, so the rest can be constructed in the dry? This, of course, is becoming more of a reality with timber frame houses.

I feel that often the children come up with much better ideas for what to test, and what is worth testing, than the ideas I have. They also have many more ideas of things to test than I have and, of course, the suggestions, ideas, thinking and doing are most appropriate to their level of thinking and the way they currently explain things to themselves. In the ideal world there would be plenty of apparatus available for the children to use, but good equipment with no ideas can be wasted equipment. So I feel it is the generation of ideas that is the first priority. With young children it is often possible to improvize, and in fact this can be an asset, in that making the apparatus is a good problem solving activity. With older children a much wider range of equipment for their more sophisticated ideas is important. However, improvization from everyday materials does something for the demystification of science — that science is only something done with vastly expensive equipment in far off laboratories — and shows that real, valuable and worthwhile science can be done with everyday objects and by ordinary people!

I eventually realized that to cope with the flood of ideas, there could be a better way if I managed to convey to the pupils that the teacher need not be the only valuer of ideas. This is where class or group discussions of ideas is useful. I set out to involve other pupils in the process. Some children have learned to argue a case extremely well! The pupils also realize that when they can discuss and justify ideas, they can take greater charge of and direct how things go and then take a much greater interest and get really involved, almost becoming self-generating in science work. So cooperation, sharing and developing together are the order of the day. Eventually, pupils can come to an understanding of valuing their own ideas for themselves, which is what every scientist has had to do to maintain motivation at the frontiers of knowledge, which almost by definition, means few others will understand, let alone be able to value, for a long time. Encouragement of imagination is also an important element as in many major advances there had to be imagined a connection, relationship or explanation which on testing was found could be proved.

Another change in my classroom practice is to be a lot more open and flexible, and less rigid and worried about achieving intended outcomes. Planning is seen more as thinking of options, which includes trying to anticipate the sorts of responses and kind of explanations that will occur and the demands that might arise. Often better ideas come up which I follow and abandon my intentions.

In the above, however, the question can be asked about how it is possible to prove the value and worth of following these ideas. Worries and pressure about aims and objectives, assessment and appraisal are frequent in teachers' minds. The reasoning behind the child-centred philosophy, the non-socially constrained, dynamic, and constructivist view of knowledge and generative view of learning are helpful here. However, I have found that getting to grips with, making conscious, having a great familiarity with and understanding the use of, the so-called science processes in practical situations has been most useful. In the early days, reflecting in some depth on what the children had done in relation to these processes was necessary, especially as often the areas to which they were applied and the results were unusual. Eventually, analysis of the processes involved in the children's activities comes easily, and the value can be made quickly explicit. One can look at what the children are doing and recognize that 'A' is reflecting, 'B' is investigating a connection, 'C' is referring to alternative sources, 'D' is planning an experiment, 'E' is applying something she has just discovered, 'F' is trying to predict the effect of a change, and so on. However, for the less familiar, I realized there are also lots of other more informal indicators of active processing in children, and give the list to date:

Informal Indicators that Children are Actively Processing

1   Children recognize in books and show you things that are directly related to what you've done in the science work, even though they are in a different form to your presentation.
2   They take an interest in new ideas in books that take them on from where you are in the progress of work.
3   They come up with lots of their own ideas.
4   They devise their own investigations that extend the work.
5   They try to work out how other or new things fit together, relate, work — i.e. critical, inquiring minds and curiosity raised.
6   Enthusiasm for getting on.
7   How many things they bring from home that fit in with the work.
8   How many books they bring from home, or from the library related to the work.
9   Increased reading of work related books.
10 They report that they have tried extra things at home related to the school work.
11 The number of questions asked.
12 Pupils who discuss and develop ideas and proposals with each other.
13 How many times the subject is raised at other times of the day. (Indicates continued thinking and personal mental involvement.)
14 Long-term interest and persistence with ideas/investigations, even long after the topic is 'officially' finished.
15 Frequent recall of past ideas that are relevant to new material i.e. they are properly integrating their ideas on how the world works.
16 Proposing possible new relationships between what is being currently done and their knowledge from previous experiences i.e. do you think that 'X' affects 'Y'?

Chapter 8:
Microcomputers in Topic Work

Joe Johnson

This chapter focuses on a number of ways in which the microcomputer can be used in topic work. Joe Johnson describes some of the work he has developed in his school in Oxfordshire, where the 480Z machine is used. However, there are equivalent facilities for the more commonly used BBC machines.

Any topic work in any primary school can include some element of microcomputer-based work which is planned to extend and enhance the interest and core work of the topic. All schools now have at least one micro and many are now recognizing that one microcomputer per class is not an unrealistic resource goal. If your own micro is a scarce 'rotating' resource you will need to plan its use within your topic work to give at least some of the children in your class an in-depth micro-based learning experience which may then be shared with the rest of the class.

If you haven't had much experience with microcomputers you ought to put your worries about them to one side and 'have a go'. Unless you have an obliging colleague, you will need to know how to connect the parts of your computer, how to turn the computer on and how to load software. All you will need to do then is to commit a little time on becoming familiar with one piece of good educational computer software and use that with your class.

There can be real opportunities for growth by children working in small groups at the micro. Groups of between two and six can work from one computer, depending on the software and how the children are organized. When a group become involved in their work the level of discussion is transformed. The problem-solving approach to cross-curricular work focuses on the need for children to develop critical skills and the computer is ideally equipped to provide many opportunities for these learning experiences.

In this chapter I shall be discussing the use of five types of computer software in topic work, which are:

(i) wordprocessors
(ii) 'tray'
(iii) logo/Turtle
(iv) adventure programs
(vi) data handling programs

These programs can be described as 'open' and 'content free'.

I shall not deal in any way with small 'closed' programs where children either singly or in small groups play a computer learning game and each take their half-an-hour turn in rotation. I classify these generally as 'plastic bag' programs since they are reminiscent of the language and maths games kept in most classrooms which can be employed as useful time fillers between the important work. Beware also that these 'plastic bag' programs can be suffocating if that is all the children are experiencing. In my own school these programs are virtually relegated to lunchtimes.

My school is a small two–class rural primary school. A new school was opened in 1975 replacing the Victorian building. The new school is set in three acres and has an outdoor learner swimming pool, a chequerboard garden, our own pet goat, Emma, who lives in a shed in a small paddock. We have also created a large nature reserve which also has a pond. We have amassed a large collection of local history material over the past seven years, which includes maps, photographs, documents, newspaper cuttings and a number of objects which have been donated to the 'museum'. We have tried to create a learning environment in which the microcomputer is a tool we can use to deepen and enhance work in any area of the curriculum.

We received our DOI research machine's 480Z microcomputer at the end of November 1982. We bought an Epson printer in 1983, a Valiant Turtle in 1985 and a Nimbus in May 1987. The software which I have been using has been written for the 480Z or Nimbus but most have their BBC equivalents. The important thing for the teacher is to become familiar, over a period of time, with at least one program in each category and make use of that to the full.

Wordprocessing

We have been regularly using a wordprocessor program with our computer at school since 1984. Using a wordprocessor, small groups of between two and four children can write together at the computer, pooling their ideas and their language skills. Children discuss language in a rather unique way. They learn from each other and develop a piece of writing together which none of the children could have written alone. The final product can be laid out in any way on the page and be printed in one of many print styles. Several copies can be printed for the children's workbooks, to be taken home and mounted for display in the classroom. Children can also use wordprocessors from an early age to give them familiarity and confidence with this new medium for writing. The use of computers, particularly for wordprocessing, may well be changing the nature of the written word by the time our primary pupils reach adulthood.

Using a wordprocessor children can:

— insert new text at any point to expand their work;
— reorder in any way or move chunks of writing anywhere in the text;
— delete any amount of work from single characters to large chunks;
— redraft their work several times to refine and perfect it;
— decide how the work should look on the screen and printer copy.

Working in groups even 5 and 6-year-olds can use wordprocessors. My experience is that the upper case keyboard does not really pose many problems for the average 6-year-old, although I do prefer to use a forty character screen, rather than an eighty character screen, with younger children.

The example below is by two 6-year-olds, who made up a story using the wordprocessor after a visit to the local fire station. They did four drafts with the teacher helping them to correct printouts which they made. The children then corrected their own work on the computer screen. Printer example 1 and 2 shows the printer being used in such follow-up work as part of a topic.

Example 1

FIRST DRAFT

Open day
anna and Nina went to the wood and we were going to pick some blakberys for mummy because she was going to make a cake for tae because are granny was coming for tae at are houes and he is going to stay the night with us. the nexst day we went to the wood agen and we saw some smock and we saw a bit of fire too and we went to the plyse stayshon it was only a cross the rowd.

FOURTH AND FINAL DRAFT

The Emergency

One day Anna and Nina went to the wood and we were going to pick some blackberries for mummy because she was going to make a cake because our granny was coming tea at our house and she is going to stay the night with us. The next day we went to the wood again and we saw some smoke and we saw a bit of fire too and we went the police station it was only across the road so that we could ring up the fire-engine. and then we went back to the wood and we got all the animals and then I went to fetch a goldfish and some water too and some rabbits. They were all hurt because of the fire and smoke and then we went back to the house because it was getting darck.

The End

By Anna and Nina.

Using TRAY

An alternative way of using the computer to enhance language work is with a program like TRAY. TRAY is a bit like photography with language or like playing hangman with a whole passage of text. The children can buy letters and predict letters and words until they have successfully predicted the whole passage. One facility allows them to keep a record of any ideas they have about the text and exactly how the text looks at each stage so that they can look back at the printouts and reflect on how they solved the text.

Following a visit to the Berkshire Downs, I made a TRAY file of John Masefield's poem, *On the Downs*. About half the class spent two afternoons predicting the poem. The quality of discussion about the poem, with its magic and mystery, was good and it led to some excellent poems being written by some of the children.

Example 2

Up On Old Humpy

Up on old Humpy
It's so windy,
But your heart
Seems to warm you with joy.
Up there on your own you feel like
A Roman marching to war,
Or a Viking going to his ship.
You want to take off
And fly up so high.
The four wheeled monster
Goes round the field,
Cutting up memories of long ago,
Up on old Humpy.

By Stephen Humm

Example 3

Preparation of John Masefields poem for TRAY

```
—  — —— ——— ————  ———  ———‒————  ————————
————_, —————————  ———  ————_.
——— ——————_‒———  —————  ————  —————  ————
————_, —— —————— ————————  ————_.
——  ———  ——————————  ——  ————————  ——  ———  ————_
————————; — ————— —— —————  ————————  ————
————— ———  ————_,  ———————  ———————,
——— ——— —————————  ————_.
———— ——  ————————  ————— ——  —— ———  ————_,  ——
————— ————————— ———  —— ———  ————_.
————— —————— ——————— ——  ——————  ————
——— —————— ——————  ———  ———————  ——  ———  ————
————_.
——— ——_‒——— —— ——— ————_,  —— ——— ————_,
——— ————_,  ——— ———————_,  —— ————— ———
———_,  —————————————— ——  —————— —— —— —————_.
—— ——— —————— ————————  ————_.
```

'On the Downs'

Up on the downs the red-eyed kestrels
hover, Eyeing the grass.
The field-mouse flits like a shadow into
cover, As their shadows pass.
Men are burning the gorse on the down's
shoulder; A drift of smoke glitters with
fire and hangs, and the skies smoulder,
And the lungs choke.
Once the tribe did thus on the downs, On
these downs burning Men in the frame.
Crying to the gods of the downs till
their brains were turning And the gods
came.
And to-day on the downs, in the wind,
the hawks, the grasses, In blood and
air, Something passes me and cries as it passes.
On the chalk downland bare.

Logo

The above examples are particularly good for developing language skills. The next activity offers a unique opportunity to let children design and invent shapes or objects which demand considerable mathematical thinking. My school has been using ARROW, the 480Z program written within Oxfordshire LEA. The small arrow on the screen is given instructions and draws shapes, patterns or pictures on the screen. The program will also drive a Turtle, a small floor robot which draws, usually on a larger scale, on paper taped to the floor. Constructing and writing logo programs which will draw even simple shapes is a complicated process.

Children have to organize themselves to solve a problem, which might be to draw a square on the screen and dependant on their maturity, ability and experience will tackle the problem in various ways. What children realize is that a 'problem' is usually a series of smaller problems which they can systematically work through to solve the whole 'problem'. ARROW is useful as a mathematical tool and part of the early experience of using ARROW would be drawing various shapes but its use can be extended into topic work.

The first example that I shall use comes from a topic on transport. Three third and fourth year girls wanted to draw a lorry on the computer. They began by trying to draw the lorry all in one go but realized that it was too unwieldy. They then concentrated on getting one bit of the lorry correct and over the period of a week completed a number of small ARROW programs which joined together to become a lorry and a van.

The programs were; CAB, which drew the cab of the lorry; TRAILER, which drew a low loader on the back of the cab; BODY, which drew a van body joined to the cab; LINE, which decorated the van body with lines; LOGO, which placed a logo on the van body; WHEEL, which drew the tyre; CWHEEL, which placed the tyre in the correct position for the cab; TWHEELS, which placed the tyre in the correct positions for the trailer and van. Lastly OFF moved the arrow on the screen off the screen so that it did not spoil the picture.

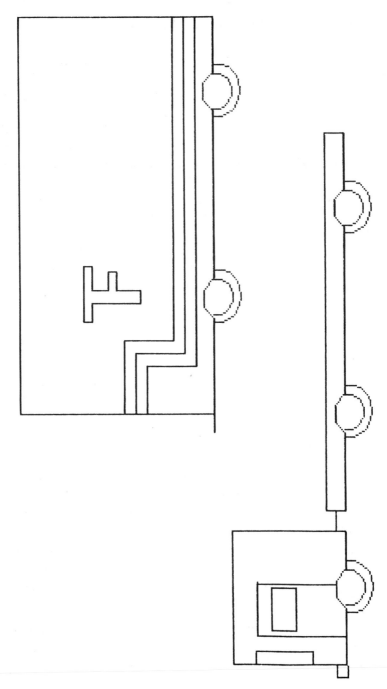

Example 4: Logo design for lorry.

Adventure and Simulation Programs

These types of computer software programs offer children the opportunity to be somewhere they're not. Simulations like *Mary Rose* allow children to hunt for the wreck in the Solent in a computer planning and problem solving simulation which can form the basis for a class topic. We have been using a suite of programs, HAZARD and RESCUE. HAZARD enables children to write their own computer adventure programs. RESCUE enables the children's adventure programs to be played as a cooperative problem-solving game. RESCUE comes with a spaceship game where the children have to explore a spaceship to rescue the professor and recover a secret formula. The children can take equipment with them to overcome the problems which they will meet in different rooms in the spaceship. As an illustration of the potential of writing your own adventure programs here is a printout of a 'game' called jungle.

Example 5

> Our RESCUE adventure takes place in the Amazon jungle. The Amazon Jungle is made up of twenty-six locations. The locations are joined together by jungle paths.

The story so far:

> Your aeroplane crashed at night in the Amazon Jungle. Natives came and stole your radio, which you need to summon help. Two people on the plane are injured and need medical help.
>
> You know that somewhere in the area there is a Doctor so you must find him urgently. The Jungle is full of dangers so you'll need to be very careful. GOOD LUCK!

When you play our adventure you are in the Amazon Jungle. You start at the aeroplane. To finish your task you must find Doctor Johnson and the shortwave radio and then return safely to the aeroplane.

During the adventure you can use the following equipment:

machete
tree spikes
hammock
oil lamp
waterproof coat
umbrella
stilts
heat sensor
shell necklaces
box of knives
rope
medicine bag — which will be somewhere in the Amazon Jungle
crutches — which will be somewhere in the Amazon Jungle

There are five problems:

(i)   A tangle of Lianas can be dealt with permanently using the machete or tree spikes, and can be detected using the stilts.
(ii) Mayapo Hunters can be dealt with permanently using the shell necklaces or box of knives, and can be detected using the tree spikes or heat sensor.
(iii) Torrential rain can be dealt with temporarily using the waterproof coat or umbrella. This problem will only occur in the jungle.
(iv) A jaguar cannot be dealt with. This problem will only occur in the jungle.
(v)   Army Ants can be dealt with temporarily using the tree spikes or hammock or stilts or rope, and can be detected using the heat sensor.

There are two traps:

(i)   If you have been bitten by mosquitos you must wait until someone brings the medicine bag.
(ii) If you fell into a pit and broke your leg you must wait until someone brings the crutches.

There is a hidden jungle path from inside the cave to the temple. It can be detected using the heat sensor. There is a hidden jungle path from behind the waterfall to near the waterfall. It can be detected using the waterproof coat. There is a hidden jungle path from the abandoned village to the jungle. It can be detected using the machete. There is a canoe from the village to the riverbank. There is a canoe from beside the swamp to the riverbank. There is a canoe from the riverbank to the riverbank.

Example 5: Map of Adventure locations

```
 1  2  3      4  5

 6  7  8      9 10

11 12 13     14

15 16 17 18 19 20

21 22 23 24 25 26
```

Location:	1	near the pool		14	on the rope bridge
names	2	the jungle		15	the aeroplane
	3	the riverbank		16	the jungle
	4	the riverbank		17	the clearing
	5	the jungle		18	near the clearing
	6	inside the cave		19	the riverbank
	7	behind the waterfall		20	the village
	8	near the waterfall		21	the jungle
	9	the riverbank		22	the jungle
	10	the riverbank		23	the abandoned village
	11	the jungle		24	the jungle
	12	the jungle		25	the maize plantation
	13	beside the swamp		26	the Temple

Inspired by a school television programme about Egypt a second year boy wanted to make up his own game about Egypt. Two other children joined him and they began work on their game. They realized as they were planning their game that they knew little about Egypt so they sorted out some books and each took some home to research. The next day they began work on their adventure game which was set in a pyramid where the players had to overcome the precautions of the pyramid maker to reach the Pharaoh's treasure. In the process of writing their adventure they had learnt a lot about Egypt and pyramids. Once they had tested it, other children were able to play their game on the computer. On a similar project my infant teacher wrote an alternative simpler pyramid adventure game which the infant children used to learn about pyramids. All the adventure games that have been written in our school form a growing resource of these games which our children use.

Information Handling

Information handling programs serve a very different purpose from the programs mentioned so far. They form a versatile tool for the exploration and understanding of information by primary school children. By using them children can manipulate information in all sorts of ways and then make a printer copy for further discussion and analysis away from the computer.

We use the EDITOR and QUEST programs to construct data files and DISPLAY and RELATE to print out graphs, pie charts, scattergrams, etc.

I shall focus on my children's explorations outlining some specific topic-based work where data handling programs have been an integral part of the resources for learning in the school. Central to my work has been the idea that this type of work should lead to children understanding what they are doing. My usual phrase for this is 'getting behind the figures'.

Measuring Topic

The children began this topic by measuring their height, weight, hand span and foot length. They each combined all results for their year group into a table showing all their names and measurements. The children went on to measure all the children in the younger class. This information was then handled in different ways. Graphs and histograms were drawn and labelled. Ordered lists were made and some older children made pie charts. As part of this general work three fourth year girls used the computer. First of all they prepared the information to be entered into the computer. I showed them how to operate the EDITOR program, although at that stage they really had little idea of what was to happen to the information once it had been typed in.

They worked very hard typing in the information which magically became 'data' and I spent part of the lunch break correcting one or two obvious errors in the data file ready for the children to use in the afternoon. We loaded DISPLAY and then our datafile which the children had called 'school'. The children discussed what to display and they decided the heights and ran into their first problem.

The computer could not handle a huge number of separate columns and lumped single entries together as others. Obviously this was not very satisfactory and the same thing happened with the pie chart. However, we had already done some grouping of information in our work in the classroom and so the children were able to understand and use the facility in DISPLAY which can put the data into different groups which were under the control of the children. The children now used the printer to print different bar charts, histograms and pie charts. They were able to print several different bar charts and compare them directly against each other.

They could now alter the number and width of the groups and they talked excitedly as they explored this new dimension in their learning. The conversation of that small group was reward enough: What would happen if I did this? How was that one different from the last one? The shape is different, why? The children were making hypotheses then testing them because they had the courage to verbalize with each other and build on each other's thoughts and ideas. They were immersed in this activity for some time.

The following term I decided to collect the same measurements as the term before, with a longer term view of collecting this information every term. This would eventually enable older children to draw profiles of different aspects of their own growth.

I brought the same three fourth year girls back to the computer and let them re-examine their 'school' datafile and print off several bar charts, histograms and pie charts.

The new set of data was added to the first file and we discovered several inaccurate measurements which the children had made the previous term. How could a child's hand span decrease by four centimetres in a term? Human error was the answer! This group also dabbled with RELATE and printed scattergrams showing relationships between height and weight and combining lines showing averages, again noted down from DISPLAY, they could make a short statement about different children as represented by dots on the scattergram. For example: Paul is below average height and above average weight. Lisa is above average height and below average weight. Paul, as you might surmise, is thickset and Lisa is tall and slim. Several other children were interested in the activity around the computer and later on the girls passed on some of their skills in using DISPLAY to other children in the class by 'piggy back' learning.

This scattergram, made using RELATE, compares heights and weights of children in the school. I have drawn in lines showing the averages for both also taken from a DISPLAY printout and marked the crosses which represent Lisa and Paul's measurements.

The computer did bring something new to this situation. It made it possible for the children to see the information organized in a variety of ways under their control, quickly! Using the computer meant that they were free from the physical chore of using paper, pencils, ruler and pen. They could concentrate on thinking about the information.

100 Years Ago Topic

Another instance of encouraging children to collect and interpret statistics occurred in a topic with a historical bias. I took the children to our local churchyard and asked them to note down the particulars of any of the gravestones of people who had died between 1884 and 1914. I had, of course, received permission from our vicar and carefully directed the children not to wander over the newer part of the graveyard. Within as many minutes a list of twenty or so people had been obtained. We combined all this information and all the facts we knew into a data file constructed by a small group of third year juniors.

With some parent help I had already prepared a QUEST datafile of

Example 6: Scattergram showing children's weights and heights.

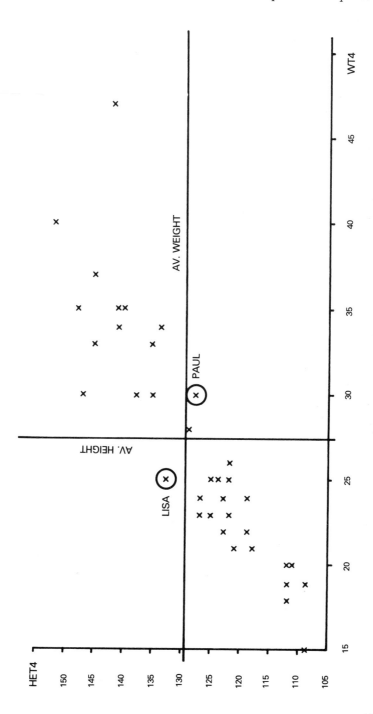

the 1881 Census of our village and two fourth year children used QUEST to see if any of the names from our churchyard appeared on the Census records. Surprisingly only four names coincided but fortunately two of the names Dandridge and Wood had relatives still alive today. The children were able to talk to them at our Senior Citizens Club which is held in the school hall fortnightly on a Thursday afternoon and this led to further investigations.

It is as well to mention that the topic also led the children to examine other sources of historical evidence. The children used copies of the original census sheets, documents which should be available wherever possible. Census data on the computer looks very antiseptic compared to copies of our local enumerator's record sheets written in 1881. Philip Hickman, our enumerator, was landlord of the *The Black Horse* which had been a beerhouse since the 1750s and finally closed fifteen years ago. I also know other things about Philip Hickman, I have a copy of his will, for example, and all this material adds interest to any study involving local history records.

With the large number of individual records involved, 379 people (each called a record) and eighteen pieces of information for one person (each called a field), it was not immediately possible to enter the Census data into DISPLAY or RELATE so I saved part of the QUEST data file so that I only had four fields, which would load into the display programs.

It took a little time to combine all the interesting fields so that the records would successfully load into DISPLAY but the time was well spent and the children were able to use DISPLAY and RELATE to illustrate aspects of life in Victorian Stadhampton with pie charts, bar graphs, histograms and scattergrams.

This histogram was made using DISPLAY and shows the age distribution of the 379 inhabitants of Stadhampton in 1881 grouped in blocks of ten years. The children found its shape very interesting, which led them into further investigations.

They followed their investigations by examining the top heavy part of the previous histograms and printed a more detailed analysis of inhabitants aged between 0 and 20. This led to discussion about child mortality, illness and disease in Victorian times and comparisons with life today.

Example 7: Histogram showing distribution of inhabitants.

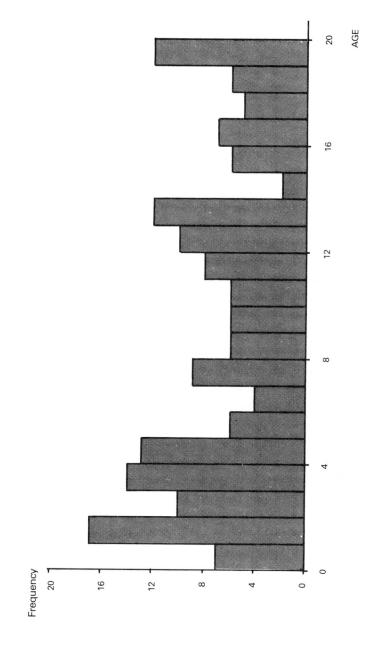

Sea Topic

This topic provided an opportunity for a further use of the computer. This time the computer helped the children to develop their questioning strategies and led them to explore ways of classifying knowledge, a vital skill, especially when children use library catalogues and book indexes.

During a recent topic on the sea I used a 'tree' program called BRANCH. Versions of this type of program exist for all school computers. Tree programs can be used by small groups and even whole classes, by both infant and junior aged children. Tree programs give children the opportunity to classify objects in the form of a binary tree which can then be used by themselves or by other children. I nearly always put up an attractive visual display when I use BRANCH.

As part of a topic on the sea the children were to spend a day on 'fieldwork' at the Marine Nature Reserve, Kimmeridge Bay, Dorset. In preparation we were studying the marine life that we expected to encounter on the seashore and in the rockpools at Kimmeridge. Fourteen children each drew a careful A4 picture of a different creature. I took these into the hall and spread them on the floor. I asked a group of six children to think of a question which divided all the creatures into two groups. They used textbooks to research and as the children thought of questions they wrote them on a piece of paper and placed them on the floor with two strips of green and red sugar paper which signified whether the answer to the questions was 'yes' or 'no'. They continued to sub-divide the sea creatures until the tree was complete. We then transferred the whole thing to a display board in the classroom then the children, in two groups of three, wrote their tree into the computer and these were saved on disc. Other children used the BRANCH tree to see if they could answer the questions correctly to find a particular creature at the end of the tree.

Our day at Kimmeridge was very successful and the sea was exceptionally calm. The preparatory work meant that the children could identify many creatures and knew something of their habitat and diet. We brought back an abandoned lobster pot, driftwood, a few pebbles, some seashells and a couple of plastic bags full of seaweed from the beach. I took a lot of photographs, including close-ups of several creatures and the only casualties were a few sandhoppers in the seaweed. The next day the whole school smelt of the sea! We carefully washed the seaweed and a group of children set to armed with books to identify different species of seaweed. When they had done this they made a branch tree of the seaweed. They were not allowed to use the colour of the seaweed as a question but they cleverly used similar questions more than once. They laid out their tree in the hall with questions and green and red strips of sugar paper leading to further questions and the seaweeds themselves. We decided not to display this tree!

SEAWEED

		Yes	**No**
1	Does it have branches?	Question 2	Question 4
2	Is it leathery?	Question 3	Oar Weed
3	Does it have thin branches?	Coral Weed	Toothed Wrack
4	Does it look leathery?	Question 5	C. Rupestris
5	Is it soft?	Sea Lettuce	Sea Belt

Some further comments are worthy of mention. Firstly this type of activity does entail the teacher investing time in preparing for data handling work. Entering lengthy data files takes time and in my opinion has dubious educational value for children. Parent volunteers have proved useful for this. The correction and organization of datafiles ready for children's use is essential to prevent disenchantment and boredom.

A number of other points need to be borne in mind:

(i) Look for opportunities in your work with children to use this resource and actively collect information which may be useful in the future (local history, weather records etc).

(ii) Seek depth of understanding for a few rather than a shallow awareness for all, this will mean giving a few children more than their fair share of computer time in the short term.

(iii) The data in use must have relevance and interest to the child.

The computer in this context is a machine which can be used as part of the process of facilitating a closer and deeper understanding of the meaning and significance of information.

Conclusion

There are benefits for children who have meaningful computer learning experiences. Some of these benefits are specific to computers and will enable those children to perceive the use of the computer as a common and normal activity as they grow into adulthood. Positive attitudes towards these powerful tools are being fostered in children now, which will be a general benefit to society. If you can't agree with this last sentence you must beware of becoming a computer Luddite! Computers also offer children new modes of learning which are difficult for teachers to set up in any other way. Notably, the quality of children's discussion, while working in groups at the computer and the way that this helps them to focus their thinking, has the potential to give these children opportunities for growth. Computers aren't as personally critical or threatening to the child as the average teacher can be. Computers don't dent a child's self-esteem in the way that a teacher can. They don't interfere but merely interact and the child generally decides the speed of that interaction. The staggering fact is that computers have only been in primary schools since 1982 and the speed of the development of more powerful hardware and software will probably lead to an information and communication revolution which could not have been imagined when the majority of the nation's teaching force were training for the profession.

IV. Recording Information

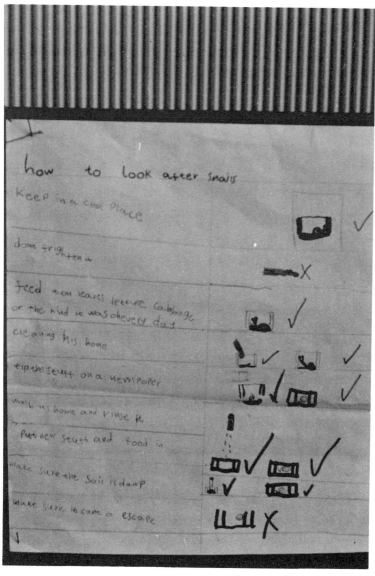

how to look after snails

keep in a cool place

done frighten in

feed eou leaves lettuce cabbage
or the kind it was ohevery day

cleaning his home

tip the stuff on a newspaper

wash his home and rinse it

put new stuff and food in

make sure the soil is damp

make sure it came o escape

Photograph 9 Charts (see p. 59)

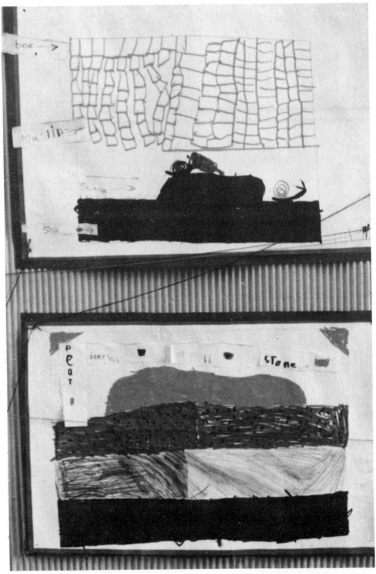

Photograph 10 'What to put in a snail home' (see p. 59)

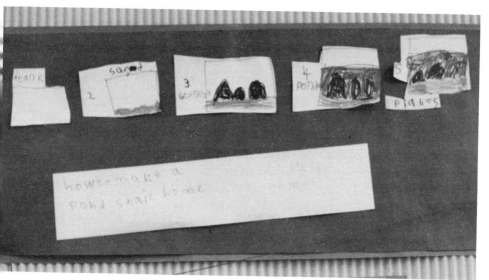

Photograph 11 Picture sequence (see p. 59)

Photograph 12 'Strength test: How strong is a snail?' (see p. 62)

Photograph 13 Individual writing and drawing (see p. 62)

146

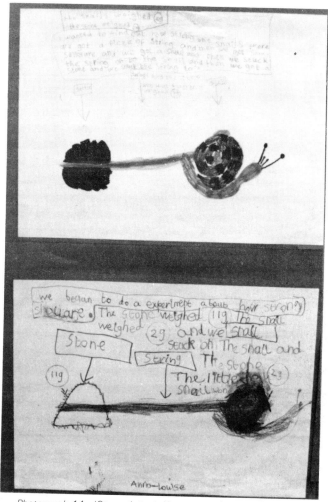

Photograph 14 'Strength test: How strong is a snail?' (see p. 62

V. Sharing Findings

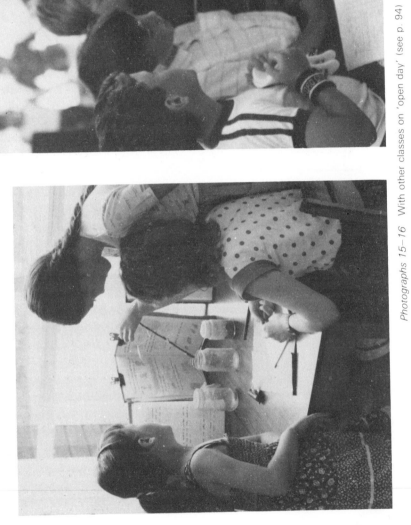

Photographs 15–16 With other classes on 'open day' (see p. 94)

148

Chapter 9:
On the Move

Simon Catling

The final chapter in this part demonstrates the preparation processes that a teacher might undertake when doing a topic. The preparation encompasses the teacher's method of planning the objectives, the activities, their sequence and also of planning how to monitor an individual child's progress. Simon Catling provides a detailed account of these stages through the example of a topic for infants with a focus on environmental education.

Children are forever on the move. In that sense the topic on journeys arose naturally. It was not, however, a topic which appeared spontaneously, but was decided on as a focus before term began. The choice was deliberate and based on a number of criteria. Table 1 outlines the reasons for selecting journeys as a topic.

The class of 6 and 7-year-olds were drawn from an inner-city multi-ethnic community. During the year they had already followed several teacher-chosen and some personally-selected topics, which included, as class topics, our families focusing on family life; people in school which extended to a more general study of people who care for and help us; animals, birds and insects which involved not only the study of pets and insects around us but also included a city farm and zoo visit; and play and games which encompassed toys, playground rhymes, leisure activities, play facilities in school and locally, and included a park visit.

In selecting journeys as the initial topic for the summer term, it was felt important to continue the shared experiential focus, to draw further on the individual contributions from which others could gain, to provide an opportunity for moving beyond the locality (though

Table 1: Criteria for the choice of 'Journeys' topic.

1 Part of children's natural experience
2 Talk about journeys, from the everyday to the exotic, had arisen in the children's conversations from time to time.
3 Journeys are an important part of all our lives, made for a range of reasons; it is worth examining why and how we make them.
4 The study of journeys offers opportunities to develop a range of experiences and understandings of a variety of ideas, skills and values.
5 It provided common ground as a class-focused study, since we all make journeys, not just the people in our class but everyone; it is a shared experience to be tapped.
6 It offers exploration of the factual and the imaginative, and the use of a wide range of resources.
7 It provided a means to move beyond the local and parochial into the wider world.
8 It provided a suitable vehicle for the development of the environmental education area of the curriculum, and could involve work in other curriculum areas, including language, movement, science, drama and maths.
9 It built on previous studies by the children.

starting from it), and to build on a connecting thread in human experience. One connecting thread running through much previous work and experience was 'movement'. This offered such a wide range of possibilities which could lead to a diffuse variety of studies that the children might find it difficult to link them together. Because of this it was decided that a more tightly focused topic would act as a sounder foundation for the term. This could, and did, lead to personal and small group topics which were broadly under the 'movement' theme. As journeys were part of all our everyday experience and had emerged from time to time in previous work, this theme became the topic.

The choice was also influenced by a decision to incorporate work on aspects of the environment which were felt to be in need of development. Little emphasis had been given to developing children's spatial awareness in previous work. The purpose, then, was to draw the children's attention more directly to their use of the space around them and through which they moved, which a Journeys theme offered many opportunities to do.

Having decided on the topic and the initial focus within it, the need was to identify possible lines of study and to undertake some initial planning. Preparation involved a variety of activities: jotting down ideas, listing ideas, skills and values to take into account, drafting a planning strategy for the topic, finding resources, considering who to approach for help, checking the school diary to see when it might be possible to arrange to take children out of school, contacting the library

Figure 1: Central elements for study in a journeys topic

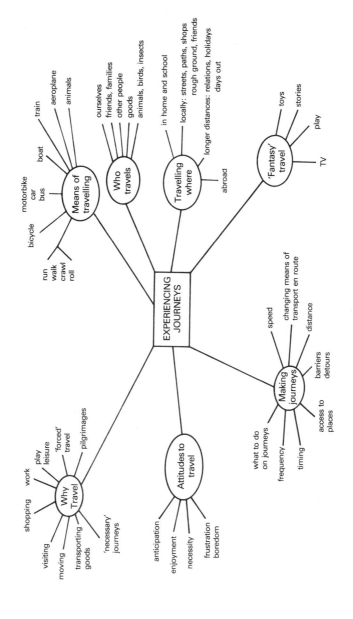

service to order books for the first half-term, walking around the local area to check for possible visit routes and sites for hazards, and so on.

The drafting of ideas and a strategy for the topic are illustrated in figure 1 and tables 2 and 3. The starting point was to note a variety of lines of study developing from the circled headings in figure 1. These were not intended to be, and in the main did not become, specific mini-topics but acted as a stimulus and could be returned to as key elements of the topic around which discussion could focus.

Bearing in mind the emphasis on the spatial dimension of journeys, a list of concepts, skills and values and attitudes was drafted (table 2). The purpose here was to identify particular concepts that would be important, likely skills that would be used, and certain attitudes and values that could be considered.

For children to build up their experience and understanding, it is

Table 2: *Some concepts, skills, values and attitudes to develop during a topic on 'Journeys'*

Concepts

Cause/purpose	why journeys are made;
Travel	how journeys are made;
Frequency	how often journeys are made;
Duration	length of time of journeys;
Distance	how far is travelled;
Accessibility	how easy it is to reach a place;
Route	the pathway a journey follows;
Barriers	what causes detours on journeys;
Mode of travel	what means of transport is used;
Movement	the making of journeys;
Migration	movement for residence from one place to another;
Origin	where journeys begin;
Destination	where journeys end;
Patterns	consistency/variation in journeys made.

Skills

Oral	talking about journeys;
Writing	describing journeys;
Decision-making	what and how to find information;
Data gathering	asking questions, tallying, observing;
Recording	pictures, charts, sets, maps;
Analysis	considering what the information might mean;
Explaining	telling others what has been found out;
Motor	drawing, modelling, moving around;
Group work	contributing personal work to a pool;

Values and Attitudes

Interdependence	depending on others when making journeys;
Care	safety in making journeys;
Concern for environment	looking after area along routes;
Anticipation	thinking and feeling what a journey may be like;
Frustration	feelings about delays and detours.

vital that ideas are introduced and revisited in terms from which they can learn. In identifying and planning a topic it is, therefore, important to be clear about what concepts, skills, values and attitudes could be developed through the topic. By this means the context and language used can be chosen to help the children to draw on their experiences. Their understanding will only grow if they are encouraged to use more searching and focused questions and vocabulary. The value in listing both 'terminology' and how it may be interpreted for the children, as in table 2, rather than just listing the terms only, lies in making clear what element of the concept or skill it is wished to help the child appreciate. For example, 'accessibility' is about rather more than just how easy it is to reach a destination, but that is the essential meaning to get across initially, which may lead to the child learning that the word 'access' is useful. In essence, the point is that by identifying key ideas as terms and meanings children's vocabulary can be extended often more quickly and meaningfully than might be thought.

Teacher-selected, class-focused topics can be planned and introduced in many different ways. Effective planning means taking account of a variety of factors. These include, bearing in mind the context of the topic in the overall work of the children, the variety of levels of development and experience among the group, educational objectives for the children, and, as a minimum, a strategy for generating the child's involvement in the topic. Awareness of the possible range of resources and their availability and potential is important too. Much of the plan may be discarded, used in other ways and changed as the children begin to develop it themselves. Nevertheless, the teacher needs to plan the initial starting points to get the topic going.

Table 3 outlines the planning strategy of the journeys topic. It identifies some of the factors taken into account in planning and the starting point for the topic study. It was anticipated that the sequence of activities listed beside A under 'starting points' would occur in the first week of term, leading into the B activities in the second week so that C group work would be under way by the third week. The display, D, would evolve as the children undertook their work, and would lead to the opportunity to talk to children in other classes about it at about half-way through the term. Such was the preparation and planning. How did it actually develop?

What now follows is an outline of the initial topic as it developed. This is presented in notes rather than prose form to illustrate the nature

Table 3: The planning strategy for the journeys topic

Context

o broader aims of environmental education in the school
o continuity of topic approach within curriculum organization

Criteria for Objectives

(a) motivation of children
(b) drawing on familiar and shared experience
(c) social skills: cooperative development and study
(d) concept and skill development
(e) developing environmental awareness

Pupil characteristics

o 6/7-year-olds
o mixed ability class
o multi-ethnic mix
o 32 children
o inner-city area
o previous related topic experience to draw upon
o variety of travel experience outside school, from limited to days out to migration from abroad
o some experience of using picture-maps and plans

Topic
Journeys

Topic Objectives

(a) to draw on personal experience of journeys
(b) to extend experience beyond familiar journeys
(c) to develop an understanding of travel and routes
(d) to examine the types of journeys people make, how, why, to where, when, with what result, etc
(e) to explore attitudes to the experience of journeys

CLASSROOM EXPERIENCE

Starting Points

A

(1) route from home to school discussion, description, drawing

(2) checking home/school route walked/driven to correct/complete description/drawing

(3) reinforcement of awareness and use of left/right/etc
— games, listening/following instructions etc

(4) use of one child's drawing/description to follow:
in groups (helper/parent) — looking for turns, features, how far; sharing, commenting on the accuracy by group

B

(5) discussion of study of route from home to school

(6) use of wall map (teacher drawn from large scale OS map) showing roads, buildings, park etc. — mark children's routes with each child

(7) introduce idea of journeys:
  (a) brainstorm for ideas to use:
    small groups working together
  (b) class sharing of ideas:
    list most common from groups single mention
  (c) small groups (self selecting 3/4 children) deciding lines of study

Group Work

C

(8) groups developing studies
— mini-topic
— methods of study
— activities/experiences
— discussion/sharing
— enquiry, recording
— analysis, reporting

(9) feedback/discussion sessions in combined groups/whole class to share findings, ideas, criticisms

Reflection: at least once each week

D

(10) presentation of group studies: class display

Resources

o children's personal experience
o experience of other people in school, at home and elsewhere
o photographs of local features
o 1:1250 OS maps of school catchment area for drawing modified map from
o arrow cards for direction game
o computer maze games
o suitable sites for visits and journeys.
o stories about journeys: to try Dahl's *Fantastic Mr Fox*, as class story (could also use *Winnie-the-Pooh* with 100 Acre Wood map blown up to mark journeys on)
o paper, felt, paint etc
o modelling materials
o copies of children's drawing/descriptions (typed) to follow
o 'getting to school': board game (own area)
o other books etc.
o resources as need arises

Adaption and Extension

Where need/opportunity arises, to intervene to develop children's experience as appropriate, including drawing individuals into a focus group, group together or a whole class input

Evaluation

(a) teacher evaluation of approach and children's response.
(b) children's reflections on their learning and experience.
(c) consideration of development into next topic

of the growth and changes of direction in the topic's life. The topic was introduced to the children during the first day of term in a general discussion. What is presented below is a sample of the development of the topic, some parts in detail, others only general outlines, and a sample of the work that was ongoing. It did not occupy all day or indeed everyday: once underway, other activities were undertaken by the children as well.

There is not space to set out the progress, hiccups, fortunes, challenges, frustration, fun had and developing understanding of each of the groups. Figure 2 illustrates diagrammatically the progress of just one group. No inference should be drawn about the depth of coverage! The study of these ideas and areas was very varied. It included writing

Table 4:   Some of the initial questions suggested by the topic

What is a journey?
What sort of journeys do we make?
Why do we make them?
Where do we go?
How do we travel?
What is it like to travel?
When do we make journeys?
Who decides we are going on a journey?
Do going to the toilet, going shopping, and going on a holiday all count as journeys?
What choices may be involved in going on a journey?
How far do we travel?
What is it like if a journey is frustrating?
How do different people react to journeys?
How many journeys do we make?
How can we find out about journeys?
Why are some journeys 'famous'?
Why do some people like travelling a lot?
Why are some people called 'travellers'?
Do we have to make journeys?
Which routes do we use, and why?

The next table shows how the topic developed.

Table 5:   Group mini-topics

3 children	Journeys to school
3 children	Journeys we make all the time
4 children	Long journeys
3 children	How we travel
4 children	Our mum's and dad's journeys
4 children	Journey toys
4 children	Canal travel
3 children	Underground journeys
4 children	Our bicycles

Figure 2: TOPIC: Long Journeys (over 4 weeks)

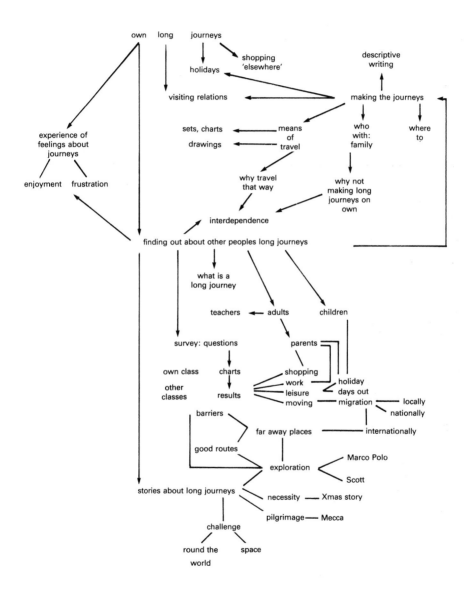

Table 6: Teacher-directed inputs.

WEEK ONE

Day 1

After lunch:	General discussion
focus:	What is it like coming back to school?
led into:	How did you get to school?
	Who did you come with?
	Did you come the usual way?
	Did you notice anything along the way?
End of afternoon:	Asked children to look at
	their route home: the way
	they went, what it is like
	— and to look again in the
	morning.

Day 2

Morning:	discussion: route to school
	Who had looked?
	What had they seen?
	Who could tell us about the way they came to school
— check question:	Which way did you turn?
	What did you pass?
— instruction:	To draw the way to school, showing the route and features (most of class)
	Small group to write about route (four children, more fluent writers)
	(into 'change' tasks as completed)
Afternoon:	Showing drawings to each other in groups of three and talked about:
	describing and questioning.
	As a class: what did they think about their drawings/writing (group)?
End of day:	Children could take drawings/writing home to check.

Days 3|4

During day:	Children to work on improving/completing
	(to their satisfaction) their drawing/writing
	Work with groups of two–four on writing two children taping their
	descriptions (one with very limited writing ability)
	Sessions in hall on both days: included moving and tuning games;
	careful listening, following instructions, some children giving directions.

Day 5

During day:	Writing and drawings displayed.
	Two groups (of three) used drawings and writing to follow to child's
	home from school (reversing route!) then back — use of helper.
End of day:	Discussion about going out and task:
	use of drawing/writing?
	accuracy?
	information?
	Comments from children in open discussion (not requested!)

WEEK TWO

Day 1

Start of afternoon:	Introduced map of area which included all children's homes (roads in plan,
	schematic home drawings, photos of some local features).
	As children worked, marked routes in pencil with each child in turn
	talking about route and referring to drawing. (later marked in felt)

response: enthusiasm (!)
             nice to see friends
             lots to tell
             got bored at home.
             walked: two by car
             parents, mum, two dads
             nothing much different, new
             road works, had to go round it.

everyone! Lots of information on everything from the shops and road works to
dogs fouling pavements.
several volunteers: three asked
some comments correcting two of the volunteers to be more accurate!

— resources ready, settled to task: discussion and checking between children.
— brief discussion about writing about the route, able to start and respond to as
  questions arose.

— wide range of styles: most pictures, some picture-maps, some detailed, others
  not.
— good! not sure if right, some wanted to check!
— most did, and brought them back
— did result in quite a lot of parental help.

— not easy to do! One child felt need to write then tape; other needs help, to
  work with individually.

— encouraged thought about left/right, and 'mirror images' — orientation.

— children who lived near each other or in same street in groups.

— much enthusiasm, comment and interest. Drawings/descriptions fairly
  accurate and useful to the children (careful not to impose adult perspective
  or expectation).

— two children said they were going out over the weekend, and volunteered to
  notice their route: both came in on Monday having completed drawings!

(prepared large scale map during previous week: several large sheets of tracing
paper!)
— interested response, and much examination of map.
  (mental note of other features to add, names, drawings or photos — children
  to draw.)

159

Simon Catling

Day 2
During day:

Continued marking routes.
Two groups out with helper to follow routes to home in morning; head in class p.m. able to take group out myself.
Began reading *Fantastic Mr. Fox*.

Days 3|4|5
During day:

Each morning, discussing other places we went to: shops, relatives and holidays — where they were, how we went there, what routes etc.
Introduced group work activities using classroom plan, and verbal instructions (written and taped) to follow round school.
— plan involved treasure hunt following a route marked
— verbal directions similar (the 'treasure' was always something to do with journeys! — book, holiday brochures, stamp, etc.)
Completed with fourteen groups over the three days.

WEEK 3
Day 2
Afternoon:

Opened with discussion about *journeys*.
Brainstorming for ideas about journeys. Listing of ideas in groups at first
— help given moving round class.
As a class pooling ideas: listed for their use.

[*Table 4* was drawn up after these sessions to put ideas into question form, as a record of thoughts both occurring to the children and suggested to them or by their ideas.]
Follow up: drawing/writing about journeys special to them.

Days 3|4|5
During day:

Children deciding on a topic to follow and who to work with, and starting on their mini-topic. [*Table 5* lists the topics chosen.]

Day 4
Assembly:

Presentation of what had been completed and found out about: personal experiences.

WEEK 4

— Use of maze games on computer by groups of children (two–three)

— Use of BIG TRAK toy for programming distance and direction — obstacle journeys — linked to drawing route to record program.

WEEK 5

— Journey to the park for 'picnic tea'.
— Use of 'getting to school' game in 'choices'.
— Visit from bus-driver parent, answering questions about her experience, also from lorry-driver parent who went abroad.
— Started reading *Winnie-the-Pooh*.
— Movement work in hall.

WEEK 7

— Coach journey to canal barge, and canal trip.
— Two groups tape-recorded parts of the day: commentary, interviews and environmental sounds.
— Photographs.
— Drawings, writing.
— Experience of journeys: similarities/differences.

WEEK 8

— Other classes invited to see the work completed by the children.
— Parents invited in as well.

— Continued interest in looking at map.
— Enthusiastic, and positively critical of the drawing used.

— Very responsive.

— Brief discussions to broaden focus before moving on, children bringing in own ideas and experiences.
— Added to experience.

— Effective in reinforcing, developing idea of direction and routes.
— Stimulated interest of children in own and other group's success (important to ensure).

— Immediately linked to experience of past two weeks.
— Not terribly successful: problems of recording in groups in short time.

— Lengthy and varied list produced.

— Range of responses: from everyday to favourite places.

— Variety of reasons for choices, e.g. underground journeys linked to *Mr. Fox*, *bicycles* to a group who had their own, *school journeys* to work already started, *long journeys* to holiday travel.

— Valuable shared experience.
— Useful reinforcement of direction.
— Developing idea of units of distance and of need for accuracy in programming. (potential work on friction of surfaces, etc. to follow-up.)

— Linked well with groups looking at parent's journeys, long journeys, how we travel.

— Booked for the idea of travel; coincidence that fitted with a group.
— Experience enthusiastically used by all.

— Lively discussion by children of what they had done with others.

and drawing about their own and family experience, discussion of what they thought and felt among themselves and with others, being read to by their parents from library books and sharing what they learnt or enjoyed with the class, undertaking surveys among one or two classes besides their own and making charts from and commenting on the data. The value of this experience lay in the opportunity to extend experience, however minimally, to use and develop new ways of expressing that experience, and to take from their 'mini-topic' a broader awareness and increased understanding of the world around them, as one would expect with 6 and 7-year-olds.

Alongside these group 'mini-topics' several inputs were made. Table 6 notes some of these briefly. The topic work of the children then moved into child-selected topics. Interestingly, but perhaps not unsurprisingly, the movement theme emerged in several individual and small group topics, for example, one based around BIG TRAK, another using LEGO, a third about body movements, and a fourth looking more directly at journeys in school building on some work in the journeys topic itself.

What was the value of this work? What were its limitations? Inevitably, teaching involves a continuous evaluation of the effectiveness of learning and experience. A summative evaluation of a topic needs, however, to focus on the question: what is it that the children have gained from the studies they have undertaken? In considering this question there is bound to be reference back to the objectives originally in mind however open-ended or prescriptive these were.

It was clear from the enthusiasm of the children, their involvement in their tasks, the way they responded to the challenges they were set and found themselves tackling on their own initiative, their increasing use of more appropriate language, and the quality of the questions they asked themselves, that much was gained. Table 7, a record of one child's 'mini-topic' work indicates what was experienced and gained. But, this is not to infer that all was rosy in the garden.

Certainly, even knowing the children well, some over- and under-expectations were made. On reflection the starting point of the topic would have been better if it had offered a limited diversity, including journeys in class, school, and to swimming as well as from home to the shops and friends alongside the route to the school. Choice would have been possible within a controlled context, and the opportunity to recognize that the same needs exist in a range of journeys. This would

Table 7: A selective record kept of one child's work in her group mini-topic on journeys

Name: Sara   *Year:* Top infant   *Class:* 8

Area of study	Interests expressed	Activities undertaken	Ideas/skills/ values	Display work	Remarks
Long journeys	Means of travelling	Writing about own experience. Asking others about how they travelled. Discussion on what 'long' means in group.	Idea of transport vehicle. Similarity/difference. Deciding on question. Consistency in asking question to sample, persistency in doing so. Tallying results.	Written description. Set drawings using pictograms grouped for duration periods. Writing about the results	The idea of a long journey not a problem to Sara until someone asked 'how far is long? — generated discussion on what to include, related to idea of duration rather than distance.
	Feelings about travelling	Taped own views from experience. Drama to show range of feelings. Parents persuaded to write down their feelings! Generated class feedback discussion. Work with Diane on expressions.	Ideas of anticipation, enjoyment, frustration, boredom. Body/facial movements to express feelings. Confidence in 'acting' in front of others.	Tape. Photographs of Sara and Diane's expressions. Writing about anticipation of a journey to a favourite place.	Generated lots of enthusiasm for expressing feelings people have while travelling — said that displays of anger/frustration based on family in traffic jams!
	Reasons for travelling	Survey of when and to where children made journeys. Helped Diane with finding out about who had moved to area.	Ideas of destination, route, frequency, migration, distance. Classifying data, interpreting data, finding places on local map.	Charts of survey results. Writing about how survey undertaken, and results. Added pictures of places to class local area map.	Extended maths work with use of simple graphs and reinforced map skills. Fascinated that some people had moved often and from abroad.

163

have meant that one less mini-topic might have emerged, but it would have given an earlier lead. The following of the everyday journey of someone on a local delivery round, such as the post round or milk round, including visits, would have been a valuable input, perhaps more understandable than the bus driver's journeys; yet that, and the lorry driver's experience, both stimulated the children, linked to particular individual experience to share, and enabled a move beyond the locality and the parochial, which was one of the objectives. Although there was a focus on the children's experience of journeys in their own studies, as one of the common strands holding the work together, this could also have formed a basis for more integrated shared experience, looking more fully at their feelings and attitudes, perhaps exploring fear and excitement alongside anticipation and boredom as

Figure 3: Journey topics in a spiral curriculum

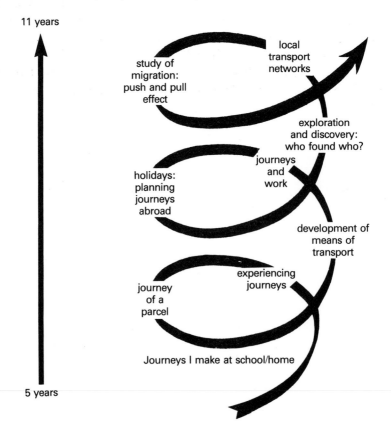

11 years

study of migration: push and pull effect

local transport networks

exploration and discovery: who found who?

holidays: planning journeys abroad

journeys and work

development of means of transport

journey of a parcel

experiencing journeys

Journeys I make at school/home

5 years

emotions experienced on journeys. The affective and cognitive dimensions could have been further explored.

There is always the danger of wanting to do everything. This topic was tackled and worked within the limits of the achievements of a class of 6 and 7-year-olds. Some were stretched on tiptoe in their learning as they reached for the next challenge. To have attempted the journeys of the post or milk, of a re-enactment of a famous journey or two (rather than encountering them), or of family migration with all its complexities would have probably created too many demands; not that enough were not already made! The essence of a spiral curriculum is that a theme such as journeys can be encountered at different points in the child's learning, each study building on what has gone before. A sequence that might develop during a child's primary schooling is illustrated in figure 3.

The conclusion to be drawn from this journeys topic is that it offers a metaphor for children's learning. The study of journeys was part of the journey in learning and experience; the children travelled its landscape drawing from it to extend their awareness of the world and moving from it to extend their horizons, hopefully better informed, more skillful, with a fuller understanding and more in control of their own developing journey. It was a medium for learning, not an end in itself.

Part 3:
Supporting Change in Topic Work

Introduction

Part 3 examines the need for schools to review their topic work policy and practice. This is in order that all staff should develop a clear understanding of the purposes of topic work and so that the children's experience of topic work has continuity and progression, as well as breadth and balance.

The first two chapters suggest that the initial step, in establishing this whole school approach, is to learn to analyze what exactly is happening in our own classroom and in each others'. Alternative ways of becoming 'teacher-researchers' are outlined and some suggestions are made as to what to focus on and how to monitor and use such observations.

The analysis of what is happening is a precursor to trying to identify the assumptions and premises upon which our teaching is based. Articulating this can help to encourage a whole staff to establish a common framework of aims and objectives — in terms of skills, attitudes, concepts and knowledge. It can also help staff to identify the range of existing teaching and learning strategies.

The third and final chapter in this part focuses on a rather different aspect. Throughout the book there has been considerable emphasis on 'skills'. This is not to underestimate the importance of attitudes and values, nor to overlook the part that topic work can play in helping children and teachers to become more aware of them. However important 'skills' may be, it is equally important to develop positive attitudes and values towards ourselves, others and the world we live in. The last chapter, therefore, is a necessary contribution to rectify any possible imbalance.

Chapter 10:
Supporting Teachers and Children
in Topic Work

Stephen Long

Stephen Long's contribution contains a review of many key aspects of topic work, in particular some alternative practices in topic work and a range of methods of record-keeping. He also reports on his own detailed case study observations of children doing topic work in a number of different schools.

During my year's secondment I was asked to carry out research into topic and project work in the middle years of education. Several questions constantly presented themselves which, because of their mutual opposition to one another, always seemed to resolve into paradoxes. Topic work, where children are actively engaged in planning and carrying out their own studies, would seem the ideal context for applying and developing a range of skills, particularly 'thinking' skills. Far from doing this, however, topic work often degenerated, both in my own classroom and in classrooms I observed during the year, into a rather uncritical quest for information amid a heavy reliance upon limited resources. I began to wonder if topic work develops children's thinking, their conceptual grasp of the theme under study and the creative use of information or is it a 'bland and vacuous' exercise where 'little of real moment can be tackled' (Lawson, 1979)?

The year's research comprised a survey of current practice within thirty-four 8–12 middle schools in one LEA. This included case studies of good practice within the same LEA and action research involving the development by children of specific skills. What emerged from this action research was the need to define what topic work is, what it should involve within individual schools and to develop ways of supporting topic work at both the school and LEA level.

The Practice of Topic Work

Whole-school Policy

All the schools case-studied had invested a great deal of time in developing whole school policies, involving all the staff. Their discussions had focused upon key issues such as definition of the work; the role of activity, first-hand experience and the children's interests; the relationship of topic work to the rest of the curriculum; the application and development of the children's knowledge, concepts, skills and attitudes through topic work; continuity, progress and record-keeping within the school; and the creation and exploitation of resources to support such work.

Central to all the schools' definitions of what each called 'study work' was the children's interest. This was seen as the principa motivating factor in the children's learning, as it had been at the beginning of this century when Dr Oride Decroly (in formulating his conception of the 'Centre of Interest') viewed it as the 'stimulus by which nervous energy is released' (Hamaide, 1925). Hence, no school directly dictated what the children studied from year to year but, through their systems of record-keeping, each teacher was able to judge what was necessary for every child to cover in terms of skills, concepts and balance of subjects across the curriculum. This highlights the central paradox involved in this kind of work: the need to balance children's interest — vital over a long-term study, with the need to ensure continuity and, above all, progression.

This raises the question of progression in what? We can fall back on HMI's description of the curriculum in terms of knowledge, concepts, skills and attitudes and, yet, still be left with the question which ones? At what age should certain knowledge, concepts and skills be introduced to the children? Both educationists and post curriculum initiatives have sought to answer these questions: Bruner (1966) put forward the model of the 'spiral curriculum' where concepts and skills, associated with specific subject disciplines, are encountered and re-encountered at increasing levels of sophistication from year to year. This model also lies at the heart of the Schools Council's curriculum development project in history, geography and social science 'Place, Time and Society 8–13' (Blyth *et al*, 1976) where key concepts are identified and study skills defined. The latter had been used as the basis for a very detailed record-keeping system by one of the schools case-studied. This involved physical, intellectual and reference skills, as well as key concepts in history, geography and science, being itemized on individual check lists. Further, their introduction and acquisition by the children was recorded from year to year. This allowed the class teachers to identify areas of neglect in the children's experience, to choose studies to compensate for this, and to be aware of the children's past achievements in detail.

In my experience such a record-keeping system is rare in any form of topic work (confirmed on a wider scale by another Schools Council research project on record-keeping in primary schools (Clift *et al*, 1981). Yet its advantages were obvious: the system had been developed by the whole staff, who therefore had reached agreement on important areas of the curriculum as well as having a broad framework within which to plan a variety of studies which were then offered to the children. Time was also allowed for keeping the records by a fortnightly exemption from assembly, yet another feature of a very pragmatic approach to solving the many problems created by an individualized study, or topic, approach to learning.

In developing a whole school policy, and attempting to resolve some of the paradoxes outlined above, it is important that it be created by the whole staff through meetings and discussion to suit the ethos and needs of the school. Publications such as *Place, Time and Society 8–13* and *Science 5 to 13* (Schools Council, 1972) are helpful but, not least because of their scope and complexity, they need to be adapted for use. The role of subject specialists to identify key concepts within their disciplines and, perhaps, relevant skills is crucial. A topic approach might ensure that their expertise is broadcast more widely and effectively throughout the school.

Only two schools in my questionnaire survey, from a possible thirty-four replies, stated that they had a post-holder for what they called topic work. No detail was given as to the roles of these persons but such a role might well be considered as part of the development of a whole school policy. I would see this person as having responsibility for learning within a school, as opposed to teaching, and to be concerned with the promotion of study or information skills across the curriculum (cf. Avann, 1985), to enable children to take full advantage of their learning opportunities. Recent research (Marland, 1981; Avann, 1983) has shown what little emphasis schools place upon the process of study and the systematic development of the necessary skills by the children. Yet this is vital, particularly as regards transfer from one phase of education to the next and, in my view, the major reason for recent criticisms surrounding topic work.

Such a post-holder should also have responsibility for the library ensuring, in current jargon, that it is 'user-friendly'. My own research revealed how much is taken for granted, where schools have a well-stocked and organized library (and most middle schools do) it is assumed that children can use if effectively. However, children need to be trained to understand how it is organized (fiction, non-fiction and reference sections), how books are classified under subject headings and how to be flexible in carrying out searches for information whether from a subject catalogue or the index of a specific book. For younger children labels with subject headings need to be on shelves and subject catalogues need to contain headings that children understand. It is no coincidence that innovators in the field of information skills, such as Pat Avann and Ann Irving, are librarians.

Record-keeping

The majority of primary and middle schools stress activity and first-hand experience as being of equal importance to the development of reading and book-based information skills. The skills associated with 'finding-out' through first-hand experience and problem-solving are perhaps more difficult to define than those which relate to the use of books. However, in developing a whole school policy for topic work the former need to be defined and some way found to record their acquisition and development by children. The skills and attitudes profile on page 181 was piloted during my year's research with a class of 10 and 11-year-old children, and covers both skills relating to empirical investigations — questioning, framing hypotheses, devising ways of testing hypotheses, observing and recording results of the test and drawing conclusions from them — and those skills that relate to the use of secondary resources and the ability to write reports from them.

The main concern was to keep the profile to one sheet of A4 paper. Each profile only covers one topic, in order to facilitate quick reference and to make the filling in (by using ticks but still indicating progress within each skill) as simple as possible. Other skills and attitudes could be added but the profile would quickly become cumbersome. The categories were developed, prior to piloting, by observing children in three different schools and noting how they actually set about both teacher-directed and self-chosen investigations relating to problem-solving in science, the use of both primary and secondary sources in history and the implementation of library reference skills on a variety of themes.

The Reflective Teacher-as-Researcher

For schools developing their own policies, and particularly defining, assessing and profiling investigation or topic skills, I would certainly recommend observing what children of all ages and abilities actually do when engaged on topic work. This could be done perhaps by an HMI style sample from each class of an able, average, below average pupil and one receiving section 11 help. A larger sample might include both a boy and a girl from each category. Such a starting point for developing a policy would mean teachers becoming researchers in their own classrooms, stepping back from their teaching and looking objectively at its effects from the children's point of view. Simple observation schedules could be devised relating to the way children tackle problems, the skills that they both display and appear to lack, and the reasons behind their successes and failures. Such data could then be used and analyzed in staff discussions and a picture created of work going on in the school from which development could be planned. Too often, in my own experience, staff meetings on curriculum development have led nowhere because of the differing perceptions of what was happening in the school in the particular areas under discussion.

Not only does the question have to be asked whether children have the skills to carry out the school's perception of topic work effectively, but also the equally 'difficult' question of whether teachers (a) know what these skills are; and (b) have acquired them themselves. Both Southgate *et al* (1981) and Avann (1983) suggest that few teachers have acquired them and that, at best, most have only a vague conception of what they might be. This is quite likely to be a factor of both their own education being predominantly content-based and their initial training being geared to subjects rather than the processes involved in learning.

Nowhere in my own training as a PGCE student in the mid-seventies was I 'trained' to carry out topic work, despite having to do so on teaching practice. It seemed to be assumed that I must already have sufficient study skills and could therefore teach about it.

Both Bassey (1978) and Leith (1981) discovered that at least 15 per cent of curriculum time in primary schools was spent on topic-related work. My own recent survey of 8–12 middle schools found that between 25 and 50 per cent of the week was devoted to the myriad forms of topic work. Such an emphasis should add weight to the argument that study, information skills, learning how to learn, topic work (call it what you wish) should form an integral part of initial teacher training. The recent explosion of information and the demands of such necessities as updating skills and retraining require citizens of the future to be flexible and adaptable in their ability to learn.

If teachers are neither really aware of these skills, nor are proficient in them themselves, then both the school and the LEA have a need to remedy the situation. Developing a whole school policy is in itself a problem-solving activity and could certainly be carried out as such if data on what children do in topic work, and the strategies that they use, is collected, analyzed and conclusions drawn from it. If needs within the school can be identified then both school and LEA based in-service training could result, especially with the new GRIST provisions now in place. Such support is vital if initiatives are to be encouraged and worthwhile change be brought about.

This has already happened in some LEAs as regards topic work. For example, in Coventry Pat Avann's work included the creation of a task force of teachers who were eager to implement and evaluate innovatory teaching of information skills. She also conducted an in-service course which both trained teachers in the skills and attempted to support work on formulating whole school policies in their implementation. This work came about through research for an MPhil degree.

A further example comes from Humberside where the LEA have

supported a major initiative from advisers on developing children's thinking through topic work. They have instituted an in-service course dealing with a whole range of issues, including skill and concept development and inter-school liaison. This has been supported by full-time secondments to the local college of higher education to further develop the initiative (Steward, 1987). This suggests that there is great interest in developing topic work so that it can fulfil its potential as a method of both teaching and learning. Secondments, such as my own, are worthwhile if they lead to liaison between the varied initiatives within the education system and to the setting up of relevant, worthwhile in-service courses.

Observing the Development of Children's Skills

Observing what children actually do when engaged upon topic work, as has been suggested above, can be a starting point for the development of a whole school policy and any ensuing in-service training. Part of my own research took the form of such observation and concerned itself with children's use of the library and their abilities to access, extract and make use of information from reference books. Some schools would certainly take the view that such activities have little to do with real topic work. One of the case-studied schools declared in its policy document that their conception of a 'study' had nothing to do with children choosing a theme at random and copying or paraphrasing reference books. Other schools would perhaps want to include the use of reference books as one of the objectives in their topic work. I would argue that developing higher-order reading skills must be one of the priorities, not least from the point of view of children coping with the demands of the secondary school and the sheer abundance of printed information in our society. Topic work would seem to be one of the contexts within which this might be done.

Sayer (1979) has suggested that instructed topic work does not necessarily lead to the acquisition of higher-order reading and research skills. (In fact it was found that secondary school pupils being taught through traditional subjects had acquired the skills to a significantly greater degree.) I was, therefore, keen to find out whether in carrying out self-chosen research topics, children used reference skills that they had been introduced to and what difficulties, if any, they experienced.

The children, a group of eight mixed-ability 11 and 12-year-olds in their final year of middle school, were introduced to specific research skills by way of the SRA research lab which provided both structured and open-ended research exercises. I was also interested to discover whether the skills would transfer from the structured to the open-ended contexts when, finally, the children were able to carry out their own self-chosen research.

Apart from the fact that almost none of the skills transferred, a number of other interesting issues arose. Because the children were aware of the names of the skills that they were attempting to acquire and apply, (this was made plain in the structured part of the work and through their awareness that I was keeping a skills assessment profile for each of them), we soon developed a common language to describe the problems that were being encountered. Being able to describe and discuss problems was obviously a prerequisite of solving them! Through observation, and here the skills profile was an invaluable tool, it became clear that the children were inventing strategies. Some of these, in the long-term were quite harmful, as they resulted in children not using skills where they were either perceived as difficult or when they had not really acquired them. The following observations were collected, along with much other data on a whole range of skills, by means of observing children working, discussing with individual children, tape-recording individual and group discussions, as well as from analysis of the final reports that the children wrote and their research notebooks.

Focusing the Search

Having been used to carrying out their own research under broad, and often vague, headings these particular children found difficulty in focusing their investigations. All embracing titles were found to be a hindrance rather than a help when they began their search for information. Consequently a period of refocusing took place after rather fruitless preliminary investigations. Hence, an interest in 'Flowers' became 'Comparing mountain and desert plants', 'Rabbits' became 'Rabbit senses' and 'Monkeys' became 'Old and new world monkeys'.

Library Skills

A short, informal test to gauge the children's ability to locate books in the library suggested, as stated before, that teachers cannot take competence for granted in children of this age and, presumably, of a younger age. When asked to find a specific book in the library all the children, except one, made a completely random search. The latter was aware of the primary subject index, was aware of the Dewey classification system (as all the others seemed to be when asked to return a specific book to the shelves) and proved able to use it. The others trusted to luck in their searches and were all unsuccessful despite having used that same library for more than three years. The least able child in the group, who later proved very perceptive in some areas of his research and produced a very worthwhile report, was able to locate the fiction shelves in the library when looking for a well known book by AA Milne. But he had no idea how to search for the author's name; no idea that the initial letter of the surname was used as a mode of classification on the shelf or that the authors ran alphabetically from top shelf to bottom and from left to right. Such observations point to the problems involved for some children and have implications for both instruction and library organization.

Using Indexes

All the children were familiar with using indexes and were quite competent where simple ones were concerned. As with their eventual use of subject catalogues however, they proved inflexible and easily daunted if their first search was futile. All the children needed to be instructed in how to use an encyclopaedia index (none were sure what 6 1016 in the Children's Britannica index signified). Nor were they initially aware that information might be indexed under a variety of headings and their searches tended to be peremptory. They also tended not to follow-up cross-references, especially in encyclopaedia indexes, despite plenty of structured work in the skill. Some transfer was effected in that children were often observed using indexes although when challenged their strategy was usually superficial. Classification would seem to be the key here and children need to be encouraged to think of as many headings as possible under which they might search for information.

Skimming

As a group the children appeared competent from the outset and were obviously familiar with the skill. No overt teaching was necessary although the least able child tended to skim when close reading of a text was required 'because it (was) easy'. The children needed to have a clear idea of what they were skimming for and whether this reading strategy was appropriate, otherwise they tended to read through an article or chapter from beginning to end especially when they had not defined their purpose in doing so. Although difficult to observe being used, some evidence of the skill in operation was gained from the children's notes. It seemed a vital one in the quick location of information, particularly in indexes, encyclopaedia articles and in the children's own notes when they collated their findings. Some transfer was noted again because of their familiarity with this skill.

Extracting and Using Information

There has been some argument as to whether young children (for example 8-year-olds) are capable of extracting information from the printed word in any way other than copying. I would suggest that any encouragement of copying uncritically from books is counter-productive, if not harmful, in the long-term.

Note-taking

There was no difficulty in observing whether children used this skill, both during and after our sessions, as they regularly handed in their research notebooks. It is a vital skill for the rapid collection of information but seems to depend on both the children's clarity of purpose in reading and the complementary skills of finding the main idea and identifying supporting details. Direct teaching proved necessary, even then real competence was only observed in three of the eight children. However, all the reports were written in the children's own words — although three of the children found it hard to read back over their notes. No transfer took place from the structured phase of the work at all. However the common language that had developed between myself and the children made teaching far more straight-forward, and proved a useful basis for tackling this complex but vital skill.

Using information

Research has suggested that topic work tends to stop at the collection of information whereas the use of the latter would seem to be a far more worthwhile goal than gathering information for its own sake.

All the children in the research group showed evidence of organiz-ing their material, particularly the six who had written detailed outlines. The skill was initially avoided, until my intervention, by the children. They tended to take a linear approach to the collection of information, writing it up as it was gathered rather than reflecting upon notes, reorganizing where necessary, writing an outline and then making a final draft. The skill is very much part of the process of evaluating material and is easily observable in both rough and final draft work. Success in the skill seemed to depend upon the children's initial clarity of purpose, a theme one returns to again and again. No transfer at the more complex levels of the skill was observed.

Evaluating Information

The practices in the structured phase were very questionable in terms of this skill: most seemed to be concerned with literal comprehension and, again, no transfer was discernible. Both Marland (1981) and Avann (1985) quote this as being one of the fundamental information skills and it seems much neglected in topic work. Only one of the children, whose report was a comparison of desert and mountain plants gave direct evidence of using this skill although others did so informally in discussion. The skill was 'avoided' by copying, yet exacerbated by reliance on one source of information. Further, no conclusions were drawn, or generalizations made, from the collected data.

Conclusion

The essence of developing a whole school policy on topic work would seem to be a clear identification of the aims and objectives of the work and the development of a detailed but not cumbersome system of observation and record-keeping. Skills — being the objectives in the work that would most readily be transferable from one topic to another — would seem the most fruitful data to record concerning individual children. This would also provide a basis for monitoring continuity and progression within the school. It would also serve as a basis for the development of a common language to describe and discuss problems that children encounter. Such skills need to be defined, understood — and acquired — by the whole staff and, to this end, school or LEA based in-service training might be necessary.

Figure 1: Profile of child's achievement in topic work.

NAME................................ AGE..... PROJECT...................................

ATTITUDES....		1	2	3	4
	Willing to collect resources for project				
	Willing to ask questions				
	Keen to find things out for self				
	Keen to put ideas to the test				
	Keen to keep records and observe changes				
	Willing to examine critically own results				
	others results				
	Recognizes need to learn new skills				
	Appreciates need to learn new words				
	Takes care of apparatus				
	Takes care of environment				

SKILLS......

PRACTICAL/PROBLEM SOLVING	1	2	3	4	REFERENCE SKILLS	1	2	3	4
Frame hypothesis					Define purpose				
Devise test					Choose suitable resources				
Organize test					Use subject indexes				
Questionnaire					Encyclopaedia index				
Observation Schedule					Card catalogue				
Devise recording format					Contents				
Carry out test methodically					Indexes				
Observation					Skimming				
Recording observations					Close reading				
Prepared to repeat tests					Using visual aids for information				
Reviewing fairness of test					Selecting relevant information				
Forming generalizations from results					Literal comprehension				
					Inferential comprehension				
Can choose appropriate recording formats					Note-taking				
Clear, logical writing of findings					Using variety of sources				
Prepared to redraft work					ORGANIZE MATERIAL				
					Makes comparisons				
Prepared to follow up and extend work					Classifies information				
					Analyzes information				
Cooperation with others					Evaluates information				
					Prepares plan for report				
					Clear, logical writing of report				
					Prepared to extend work and search further				

KEY
1 Cannot do at all.
2 Has some capability — with help.
3 Has some capability — independently.
4 Appears to have mastered this skill.

Chapter 11:
A Report on School-Focused Development of Topic Work Throughout the Primary Years, 5–11

Margaret Armitage

This chapter recounts the way in which a school began to examine its own approach to topic work, particularly the classroom organization. Margaret Armitage describes the way teachers, because there was a high level of trust, were able to go into each others classrooms for prearranged observation sessions.

Why Do We Need a School Policy for Topic Work?

Recent research appears to show that children learn most successfully in those contexts which make sense to them and which have realistic objectives and outcomes (Donaldson, 1978). It is also recognized that this learning takes place in an holistic, unfragmented way. For young children in particular, experience and learning have an extremely close partnership. Thus, to view the curriculum as a unit and to use the vehicle of an investigation to achieve that unity gives us the underlying theoretical basis for a way of learning and teaching such as topic work. Perhaps of even greater importance is that a common theme can provide realistic starting points for the children to define their own learning goals, plan cooperatively how these goals may be achieved, access and organise information, develop continuous evaluation skills and present the acquired information to an audience.

Wray (1985) also suggests further particular benefits which derive from topic work. He stresses that a major contribution to children's learning is the degree of motivation which can be engendered and that this can be harnessed by the teacher to create a relevant context for the acquisition and practice of certain skills. In addition, an investigation has the potential for developing children's abilities in approaching and tackling significant problems. A structured system is required in which a number of alternatives are identified, considered and tested and the results used to aid the final choice made.

It is clear that all the skills described above are those relevant to all areas of the curriculum and, ultimately, for life outside school. But they are of no value if the social skills of cooperation, discussion/debate, respect for others' opinions and group organization are not also nourished. This is where an investigation finds its true potential. It is concerned with increasing knowledge but, much more importantly, it gives the context for learning how to get that knowledge.

Whilst teachers may like to adopt a holistic approach, it is also important to remember that we must be prepared to analyze the curriculum, examine how it is defined by our philosophy and to describe clearly what that philosophy is. If topic work were to achieve its full effectiveness, then the philosophy would be seen in practice. Barrow (1981) advocates that schools should think idealistically about the nature and reason of education, since 'schooling' should be a major contributory factor in 'shaping the future as well as providing for it'. He goes on to describe the criteria for judging an educated person as:

— understanding our place in totality
— being alert and appreciative of people as individuals
— being able to distinguish between logically distinct questions
— being able to discriminate and have particular concepts with an ability to grasp complexity.

This implies that the curriculum which schools provide must have a close affinity with 'living'. It must bring children to appreciate what life is about in its broadest sense, as well as helping them towards taking an enriching and valued part in it themselves. Children will need to be able to be flexible, adaptable and have an ability to take responsibility and chances. There is also a need to work alongside others in a cooperative way, be willing to state one's own view, to recognize a problem and propose alternatives to achieve a solution, to locate sources of information and use these effectively and efficiently for one's own purposes as well as being able to make one's leisure time rewarding and self-restoring. Writers such as Stonier (1982) speak of the growing need for education to meet such objectives: for example for employment, for life (i.e. learning how to live), for the world, for self-development and for pleasure.

> In the future, obtaining and organizing information will become the dominant life activity for most people. What one enjoys learning most, one learns best ... The new objective of education will not be to educate for uniformity, but rather for versatility and diversity ... This, then, is the challenge to education; to understand what is now happening to our society, and to respond to it imaginatively and most important, effectively.

Are we really anywhere near these goals? In general, I think not. We have placed too great an emphasis upon learning facts and the end product rather than seeing the process as being the crucial factor towards true learning. There has been little concern about concepts and key skills — only upon the content with little regard to development either within or between schools. Further, the question of development has tended to be overlooked. However much individual teachers promote a true child-centred approach none of it will be of lasting worth unless there is a continuity of approach throughout the school.

I am fortunate to have extremely gifted colleagues who, individually, stimulate and interest children in a rich variety of ways. However, we had not combined our expertise to produce the needed consistency in themes, skills or concepts or in approaches to learning. This does not imply that a 'syllabus' or a 'straight-jacket' was required but we did need to share our expertise, discuss common problems and try to find a way together to come to a broad understanding of the term 'topic work'. Colleagues had expressed a desire to discuss our policy on a number of curricular issues. However, a starting point for concentrating upon investigational aspects had still to be found.

INSET Developments on Investigational Work with Colleagues

Our Existing Work

The first step was to find a starting point for a discussion with colleagues about investigational work — to consider our present good practice, to share ideas on how such work is begun and developed and, more importantly, to debate the reasons why we promote this form of curriculum. From discussions on the nature of the work, I hoped that we would collectively create conditions for more concerted, coordinated and continuous ways of developing investigational work supported by valuable and purposeful systems of recording. Tackling a common problem would also help the staff to share their obvious expertise.

There is good practice already in existence and it was essential that this was recognised and shared. In summary, the following aspects are evident in the school:

— topics are undertaken which stimulate and motivate children;
— themes are appropriate for the age of children;
— topics are integrated with other areas of the curriculum but not at the expense of sincerity;
— science is often an integral part;
— excellent art work is achieved using varied techniques;
— valuable displays are created;
— many opportunities exist for the children to share their work with the rest of the school;
— teachers conscientiously plan using a wide variety of resources;
— out-of-school visits are an essential nucleus;
— major emphasis is upon practical experience;
— parental participation is encouraged.

My Personal Role

I was determined that whatever form the meetings took, my role should be that of enabler and coordinator. I aimed to try to adopt the role as described by Gray (1982) with reference to the climate necessary for INSET development within schools:

It is characterised by openness towards colleagues and a willingness to share, a preparedness to confront others when a concern is felt, a willingness to work through problems however difficult and uncomfortable, a readiness to accept responsibility and be committed to others, and a disposition towards being supportive and encouraging of colleagues.

In essence, I wished to create opportunities in which my colleagues would feel able to express honest opinions in a supportive atmosphere and in which they would be full collaborators in defining our policy. These are, of necessity, demanding and perhaps idealistic goals and, as Easen (1985) warns, this way of working may not only 'generate new alternatives for action but it also increases vulnerability'. Our inner values are difficult to explain and if these beliefs are challenged we feel threatened. If any lasting change were to be made in the practice and in teachers' attitudes, then any plans I made must encourage colleagues themselves to want change as well as collectively form methods to enable that change to take place.

Plans for Implementation

The starting point

Patrick Easen's book (1985) helped greatly in considering the scale of the problem and possible ways of tackling it.

The difficulty was to find the initial spark for working with colleagues towards examining and evaluating our practice. I was reluctant to be seen as the sole initiator because if my colleagues did not feel the need to investigate what we were doing in topic work then they were likely to be reluctant to change if I were to impose my views on them. However, the problem of finding the starting point was easily resolved.

A colleague had attended a science course and had given me a sample of a topic record sheet from another school. She asked if something similar would be useful for our school. I discussed with her the implications and possibilities of starting some meetings to talk about topic work and she was most excited by the prospect. She also felt that the rest of the staff would welcome the opportunity.

I raised the matter with colleagues informally on an individual basis. Again, all responses were positive and I then felt enabled to consider how we might approach the issue at the beginning of the summer term.

Many of the ideas for the conduct of our meetings derived from a series of meetings which I had been privileged to attend. These were organised by the local primary adviser with a group of seven head-teachers and the senior schools adviser. The insights I had gained into how groups work and into children's learning were of inestimable value. I decided to base our meetings on the following principles:

Aims:
- (a) to open discussion on investigational work;
- (b) to share experience and expertise;
- (c) to begin from current good practice;
- (d) to share concerns and hopes.

Objectives:
- (a) sharing of topic work starting points and planning methods for this term's theme;
- (b) addressing the question 'What do I hope the children will gain from the work'?;
- (c) sharing concerns about the nature of the task;
- (d) making plans for particular areas to be discussed in depth at future meetings.

Staff meetings

In all my early planning, I was particularly conscious of the need to allow a great deal of flexibility. If the curriculum changes were to be effective and lasting then colleagues must be involved at all stages and decide what and how matters were to be discussed. Therefore, the process must be a dynamic one although I felt a general strategy could be drawn up to help focus our thinking. The above objectives were submitted to each colleague and an agenda was offered for their reactions in the week prior to the first meeting.

One member of staff made the valuable suggestion that some of the initial sharing of concerns could be done in pairs before the meeting which might give us more time to concentrate on the implications of the results. I felt this was an excellent idea and so amended the agenda (appendix A). Again this was circulated well in advance of the meeting.

After the meeting a record of its progress was completed in the form of a chart, as shown below. A summary of the main outcomes was also made (appendix B).

Strategies	Procedure	Comments
Sharing present. plans and procedures.	Brief report from each colleague.	Good sharing session. Concerns and problems were also raised at this stage. Valuable insights into different planning tools. All were involved fully.
Sharing thoughts on the purpose of topic work.	Brainstorm 5–10 mins. Write ideas on cards.	All major aspects covered. Showed deep thinking and awareness of issues. All colleagues contributed.
Sharing thoughts on the purpose of topic work.	Classify these ideas, for example language/ study skills, social and intellectual skills etc.	We found this quite difficult but all helped sort into categories. Made easier as points were written on separate cards so they could be shuffled around.
Sharing concerns.	Brainstorm — then classify problems.	This was done prior to the meeting. Very supportive atmosphere. Uncomfortable yet crucial issues raised.
Ordering priorities.	Staff discussion. from activity 4 to break major problem into manageable parts.	Very cooperative. Major concern was seen to be 'organization'. Two outcomes were: to observe own classroom and visit each others.

A very exciting development occurred at this meeting. A colleague suggested that we choose a day in which we would take particular note of groups engaged in topic work, record the problems that arose and, as this had been identified as a major priority, focus our attention upon our own classroom organization. The implications could then be shared at our second meeting. This was a most positive move for it would certainly mean us having to be very honest and open.

I then made an additional suggestion that perhaps it might be useful to visit each other's classrooms whilst the children were engaged in their activities. I was delighted that colleagues accepted this proposal with enthusiasm. Following this session, I discussed with the supply head how we might organize INSET class visits in our own school. The proposal was mentioned to the local primary adviser who gave us two full days supply cover. Colleagues were free to state which class they would like to observe and a programme was drawn up.

I also spent some considerable time thinking and talking with colleagues about the best way to structure our second meeting, where we had agreed to report back on the observations which we had made in our own classroom. This was in order to avoid it becoming entirely anecdotal with little sharpness of thought. I felt that some structures might help us to concentrate upon the issues of topic work which had emerged from our first meeting, especially that of organization in our own practice.

Sharing our observations of our own classrooms

An agenda (appendix C) was given to the staff prior to the actual day in which we were to examine what was taking place in our classroom. Each teacher agreed to give a short report focusing on the issues identified on the agenda. The outcomes were written on large sheets.

It quickly became obvious during the discussion that what had appeared to an individual teacher to be problems which were unique to them were, in fact, shared by the rest of the staff — a reassuring occurrence. What was most remarkable about the sharing of observations was the extraordinary degree of honesty and complete openness of colleagues as they spoke of their difficulties in organization and criticized their own approaches. The very act of laying our practice open in front of professional peers, instead of increasing vulnerability and insecurity, seems to have bound us closer together for we share the same concerns.

Visiting each other's classrooms

In order to gain maximum benefit from this rare opportunity, it was felt that some guidelines for observation would be useful. Each colleague had different needs so I drew up a list of issues and questions which could be used in a flexible manner (appendix D). It was re-emphasized that the focus was organization as this had been identified, in the first meeting, as our major priority. Some colleagues wanted to observe the teacher and how she used her time, others wanted to look closely at the actual organization of the children whilst others welcomed the opportunity to observe problem-solving approaches.

We completed the whole programme of visits and a further meeting was arranged at which we could share our observations and implications for our practice. The immediate reactions seem to be that the exercise was worthwhile and may have helped to open possibilities for change.

My own, personal views on being visited by a colleague were mixed. I am quite used to having visitors but being observed by colleagues I found to be more of a strain yet at the same time more stimulating than a visit made out of context with no chance for any follow-up. However, I did feel vulnerable yet not in any way threatened. All three colleagues who made a visit took particular care not to be intrusive. On the contrary, so valuable was the opportunity to sit and watch children and teacher at work that they used the time to blend into the background.

Preparing for the visit certainly helped me to crystallize my reasons behind developing particular ways of working and the purposes of the various activities. It was a great deal easier to show colleagues how children are encouraged to debate, hypothesize, report and discuss than it is to explain out of context. I think it was particularly helpful to show the whole working atmosphere and how groups were organized so that any further discussion will be based on shared understandings. Nevertheless I do not think I was quite as relaxed with the children on one of the visits as I usually am and the children seemed to react differently to having another member of staff in the room, even though I had explained to them what and why such observations were being made.

For my own part making a visit to another teacher also resulted in particular responses. I took this opportunity to visit the probationer teacher. Part of the deputy head's role must surely be that of giving practical support to colleagues but, if the time is not given in which to see them and their children in action nor to be able to work alongside them, then any support is only in a vacuum. So it was with pleasure that I spent a morning in this teacher's class. It turned out to be a privilege. To see her working in a way which it has taken me fifteen years to recognize the value was a heartening experience.

I was able to observe two children I did not know well at one-hourly intervals. This helped to emphasize the importance of giving children time — not merely to produce something on paper but time to talk with each other about what they are doing to develop their intellectual and social skills. I could also see clearly how long the process was between starting on a task and producing a piece of writing. This was not because the children were wasting time, but like adults, they need time to collect and formulate their thoughts — which could well appear to be day-dreaming to a busy teacher. Through close observation I realized that this was a vital stage we often deny to children.

My presence did not seem to unsettle these children as mine had been on one occasion and I had no difficulty in fitting into the class routine. I found that being with an older age group extended my understanding of children's development—an age group which I shall be involved with next year. I also enjoyed the chance to work with children on an equal basis at a table where they were drawing a model boat. As this is not a strong skill of mine, they were able to give me advice and constructive criticism. Finally, seeing another method of organization was particularly useful.

A meeting was arranged for the week after all our visits were completed so that we could share experiences. Each member of staff had an agenda to help us structure the discussion (appendix E).

Development for the Future

A great deal of data has already been collected through our discussions and this will need sorting and some kind of priority list compiled. The problems we have highlighted will have to be categorized in terms of social, practical and intellectual areas and ways of examining these decided upon.

I anticipated that these issues would arise:

(a) Supporting each other as we look for ways to solve our individual problem. I felt that one obtainable objective to be reached within a reasonable time span would be less daunting than having to cope with a long list of them. Concentrating upon one might also enable us to have some success.

(b) Deciding on priorities from the collected recommendations for the school on topic work.

(c) Longer term goals will include:
— referring to the classroom analysis and deciding what it is which makes the children motivated in topic work;
— making some statement about how this can be encouraged from 5–11 years;
— how can we achieve greater continuity in the principles of topic work and are our expectations the same;
— we shall then need to return to the other issues raised at our first meeting namely finding the starting points and those concerned with methods of ensuring development of skills, concepts, attitudes and themes.

It is more than likely that such matters will take the majority of the next school year to explore fully. We also need a period of time in which to consolidate what we have already achieved. Many of our personal attitudes have been changed, other possibilities of working with the children became clear and a broader perspective of topic work created. Change cannot happen in a rush. Individual teachers need time now to experiment with the new ideas in an atmosphere of mutual support.

Conclusion

I have been particularly fortunate to be able to work with very supportive colleagues who welcomed the opportunity to raise questions relating to existing practice. Inevitably, these questions made us feel uneasy and uncomfortable at times as we had to expose our methods to other professionals. We were also often in the position of having to say that there is not one known solution. Not being able to find a ready answer to our questions can be unnerving, too, but I feel we are now in a position to say we might find possible ways forward by simply sharing the experiences we have, by trusting ourselves and the children to have a go and not be afraid of failure and by supporting each other along the path.

In all the activities undertaken with colleagues I have endeavoured to hold to the maxim stated by Easen (1985) that effective school-centred INSET has to have three elements:

— curriculum change i.e. the 'process of identifying, defining and solving problems specific to the school';
— personal change i.e. reflecting upon present practice, challenging familiar assumptions, exploring new ways of acting;
— interpersonal change i.e. 'the process of effective communication so that mutual support may be sought and given through self-disclosure and feedback'.

We obviously have a long way to go and we are new and inexperienced as yet in all these elements but at least a beginning has been made.

I have become very aware of three key elements during this term which collectively lead to successful INSET. The first one relates to the fact that teachers and their methods or attitudes cannot be changed by outside agencies but only by they themselves seeing the need for change. The second element relates to the way we learn. Just as we are endeavouring to help children learn through solving 'real problems' so it is with staff. Our INSET activities should evolve through trying to find a solution to a relevant question defined by the teachers themselves. Finally, the third element is concerned with personal change without which no INSET will be effective: personal change which requires us to make decisions about our own teaching based upon honest reflection upon the effects of methods, attitudes and approaches.

During the next year, colleagues felt a need to consolidate the thinking of the previous year. This meant that we could focus our attention on precise strategies which might achieve our goals. Some of these were practical, such as managing the classroom to encourage greater responsibility and initiatives from the children. Some were attitude-based, such as focusing on true collaboration amongst the children. Other strategies were more teacher-orientated, such as devising planning techniques which were more flexible so that children could play a more central role concerning the selection and development of their work.

We wanted to continue to support the shift we had begun to make — from a concern with the 'what' to the 'why' of topic work. For this reason we undertook to continue the following:

(i) developing purposeful collaborative discussions between teacher/children and children/children on issues and tasks selected by the children, in order to let the children initiate the ideas;

(ii) ensuring that value is placed on the processes and not just the outcomes or content;

(iii) developing an awareness of the need to harness those opportunities which are most likely to develop attitudes and skills towards learning in general rather than particular knowledge;

(iv) bringing children into the important stage of evaluating their work, so that they focus on what they perceive as learning, and how they perceive their performance in relation to those attitudes and skills identified as important by the teacher — which could lead to the negotiation of future goals.

In addition to individual teacher's strategies, the staff drew up a framework for topic planning as follows:

(i) groups of skills, attitudes and concepts were collated as a guide to possibilities;

(ii) topic work planning (previously in the form of webs which emphasized content) was extended to include objectives in terms of skills, attitudes and concepts.

This consolidation phase was necessary to give staff time to turn discussion into fruitful decisions. It has also enabled us to turn vague notions about 'self-investigation' into an integral part of our classroom practice. The work now before us is to develop more efficient ways of monitoring children's progress which will help us to plan for continuity both within and between schools. By these means, therefore, another cycle of INSET activities have already begun. During the next year, I hope we shall continue on this path towards being a 'thinking school' as defined by Easen (1985):

> A school which is able to review its operating methods seriously and undertake activities which will improve the curriculum actually experienced by the pupils is a 'thinking' school.

Appendix A

FIRST TOPIC WORK STAFF MEETING

1 Sharing present plans — a 1–2 minute explanation about any plans made for this term.
2 Why do we do topic work? — whole staff brainstorm 5–10 minutes.
3 Sorting out ideas from the brainstorm.
4 Sharing concerns about investigational work.

Please would you meet in pairs before the staff meeting and report back at this stage about your feelings. Maybe you want to concentrate on such things as, for example, organization, making changes in the way children take part in the planning, development of skills or themes, record keeping or study skills. These are only suggestions.

Elaine/Marion   Margaret/Catherine   Heather/Brenda

5 Ordering priorities for future meetings from the results of 4.
6 Decide on classroom activity or observation in preparation for the next meeting.
7 Decide on next meeting.

Appendix B1

OUTCOMES OF FIRST TOPIC WORK MEETING
Present plans and procedures

1 Media/surveys.
2 Brainstorm with children.
3 Children's interest/questions.
   Corporate decision making.
   (What shall we do?
   What do we want to find out?)
4 Continuation from previous term.
5 Immediate environment/school.
6 Children organizing the arrangements.
7 Visit from previous term.
8 Children making own topic web.
9 Things which can be handled by children.

Appendix B2

PURPOSES OF TOPIC WORK

social skills

1 Cooperation.
2 Common bond amongst class and community.
3 Independence of working as a group.

language skills

4 Prediction/hypothesize.
5 Reason for study skills and others.
6 Communication skills of all kinds.
7 Need + purpose for recording in different ways.

attitudes

8 Enjoyment/motivation.
9 Discovery of learning — excitement.
10 Real outcome — purposeful — relevant.

intellectual

11 Focus for activity and thought.
12 Broaden horizons.
13 Bringing together all aspects of the curriculum.
14 Learning how to learn.

Appendix B3

KEY CONCERNS: GENERAL

1 If left to children how to select/what basis for selection?
2 If left to the children, how can the introduction and practice of skills be covered?
3 Teacher's role in planning?
4 View of end product?
5 Children's view of the purpose?
6 How to get young children purposefully involved in planning?
7 How to get going without dictating?

KEY CONCERNS: ORGANIZATION

1 Time spent in explaining, talking.
2 Should it cover all areas of the curriculum or not.
3 What about the amount of time spent on topic work?
4 Organization of the rest of the class whilst needing to work with one group on, for example, getting information from books?
5 How much support and of what kind should the teacher give to the children in the planning?
6 If the planning given to the children, things are less predictable. How to cope with this on a daily basis?
7 How to ensure the children meet many experiences rather than following the most popular.
8 Difference of focus in teacher's planning/children's planning?
9 Planning for integrated day?

Appendix B4

PRIORITIES FOR FUTURE DEVELOPMENT

1 Record keeping of children's skills.
2 Keeping summary of themes covered.
3 Identifying value and purpose of display. Pressure of 'standards'.
4 Maintaining quality of work i.e. craft skills.
5 Involving parents.
6 Developing skills — priorities visible/invisible
7 Children's self-evaluation.

Appendix C

SECOND TOPIC WORK MEETING

Suggested outline for sharing our observations of our own classrooms and topic work

1. Brief description of the activities.
2. Intended goals for the children (what was hoped that they might learn in terms of concepts or skills).
3. Intended goals for the teacher (how were we hoping to spend our time).
4. How were the children set off on their activities (how did they know what to do?)
5. What did the children do — what were the outcomes?
6. How did you spend your time— what difficulties arose?
   — why did these arise?
   — how did you try to overcome them?
7. Summarize our experiences from the day and list some issues which we might go on to explore during the term.

Appendix D

Suggested outline for observations on 1/2 day visit to each other's classrooms.

Focus on organization arising from earlier discussion:

1 Organization of children—groups/individual/class.
2 Organization of activities:
   — how do the children know what to do?
   — degree of responsibility?
   — how are tasks allotted? explained?
   — when activity complete what happens to the group or individual.
3 Organization of resources/materials.
4 Organization of teacher's time:
   — what method of contact with children?
   — what appear to be teachers priorities in her use of time?
   — what difficulties arose for the teacher?
   — why did these arise?
   — how did the teacher overcome them?

It may prove useful to discuss with the teacher whose class you are visiting before and after the visit the following issues:

What will the teacher/children be doing (activity)
What is intended? (goals for teacher and children)
What happened? (in relation to these goals)
What were the children learning?
What were the difficulties? (for teacher and children)
What implications now arise for our own teaching and organization?

To make the visits worthwhile we need to decide for ourselves:

1 What to observe (topic work organisation).
2 Who to observe (general organization of whole class at first but then focus on a group, or a pair, or individual child or teacher).
3 When to observe — how often?
4 How to record our observations.

Appendix E

THIRD TOPIC WORK MEETING

Ways of analyzing what we have observed in each other's classrooms

Introduction: Brief description of what you observed.

1 What skills did you observe being used?
  (social, intellectual, practical).
2 How was the children's time organized?
3 How did the teacher organize her own time?
4 What were the children's attitudes — can you account for these?
5 What problems arose and why? How did the children/teacher try to overcome them?

After looking at your responses:

1 Could you make one recommendation for yourself, for example,
  (i) the main change I want to make is ...
  (ii) the problem is ...
  (iii) my particular aim ...
  (iv) my first objective is — what? how? when?
2 Could you make one recommendation for the school with regard to topic work?

Chapter 12:
Values and Topic Work

Simon Catling

In this final chapter Simon Catling illustrates a number of different values which children might acquire through topic work. Many of these are unintended and can be considered as part of the 'hidden' curriculum. They are, therefore, values to which we need to be particularly alert. These include the values attached to the individual child as a learner, as well as the value that a child might attach to other children as sources of learning. Furthermore, there are the values and attitudes that children might acquire about the validity of certain ways of learning through the choice of resources used, as well as the substantive content which the children will learn by means of the 'evidence' which those resources provide.

In the recent past analysis of the theory and practice of topic work has concerned itself with such issues as rigour (Thomas, 1982), planning (SCDC, 1985), structure (Bonnett, 1986), content (Catchpole, 1986) and evaluation (Leith, 1981). A section of almost every HMI report on schools for 5–12-year-olds considers these elements of the topic work debate. The focus, more often than not, is on the development of children's thinking (Bradley *et al*, 1985) or on skills (Wray, 1985; Avann, 1985). Less frequently is the area of attitudes in and to topic work examined (Gunning, Gunning and Wilson, 1981; Lane, 1981). All these studies are concerned with, and about, the visible topic work curriculum. What is even less explored is the hidden curriculum of topic work. By 'hidden curriculum' I mean the unintended and unrecognized messages that children pick up and 'receive' from the process and content of topic work.

This chapter explores this area of the 'received' values which children may well take away with them from the learning experiences they encounter in primary school. The purpose of the chapter is to heighten our awareness to this fundamentally important dimension in children's learning. The approach used here is to depict a number of 'cameos' that raise questions, and to offer some guidance on how we might tackle the issues. The 'cameos' should encourage us to recognize the ever present need to reflect upon the unchallenged values children draw from their work.

Working as a Group

Cameo 1

Mandy, Cindy, Rehan and Tom are working around a table. The class is involved in a topic about the Middle Ages. These four children, all aged 10, have chosen to pursue the theme of clothing, on which a wide variety of book resources are available. The class works in six groups of three to five children, with each group taking a different but related theme, and working cooperatively.

A central theme which all groups are examining is the interdependence of people in communities at that period.

Within the clothing group the children have decided to follow individual preferences: Mandy is doing ladies clothing, Cindy peasant dress, Tom clerical clothes and Rehan, armour. The children occasionally ask each other for a spelling. Sometimes they spend a few minutes commenting on a TV programme or discuss some personal news. They rarely comment on each others' work, or share what they have found out; rather, the questions which emerge are 'Is there anything in your book on...', or, 'Pass me that, looks as though the picture could be useful...'.

One avowed intention of such a class topic is that the children are sharing a learning experience and working together. However, what emerges from a situation as described in the cameo is often a very different experience, though not uncommon (see also Tann 1981 and 1987). Instead, the children work alongside each other, rather than in a collaborative fashion. The children, therefore, do not receive any positive messages about working as a group. In practice, such a situation reinforces independent learning which could just as easily take place behind individual desks. Learning might occur in a more relaxed atmosphere, but neither the task not the context enhances the development of interdependent learning. Hence the actual experience is at odds with the intended aims of developing shared responsibilities, mutual help, trust etc. Further, the children saw themselves as doing individual work, essentially presenting a collection of separate products rather than a single coherent piece of work as their group's outcomes. This lack of interdependence in their own working style is both at odds with the teacher's aim of groupwork and in conflict with one of the key features of medieval life — interdependence — which the teacher hoped they would come to understand by experiencing it themselves.

For the teacher, a key concern relates to the way in which the practice of topic work needs to be coherent with the aims. To achieve this coherence, it would seem useful to pose a number of questions in order to evaluate the working practices:

* how do I want the children to work;
* does the content they are exploring encourage them to work in a way which will complement my aims;
* when I observe them working, does it 'fit' with what I imagine should be happening;
* what do my discussions with the children about their work and the way they are doing it reveal about their actual practices — and their perceptions of it;
* what does the end product indicate about their approach to the execution of their work;
* what should I do next, how can I build on their experience and extend it, what other experiences of alternative ways of working are needed, how should I introduce them to show their equal worth and complementarity?

Resources

Cameo 2

Angela, Uzma and Sara are working on their own 'animal'

topic. Angela is involved in a study of horses, Uzma is doing dogs and Sara is looking at eagles. This work is done with the support of a well-stocked library. The topic is pursued over a five-week period. The children produce both personal files and display work, which are essentially a selection and reinterpretation of book-based information. The purpose of the reliance on the use of books is to develop the children's study skills.

The development in children of such enquiry/study skills is seen by teachers to be a vital element of much topic work (Tann, 1987). It is often for this reason that there is so much reliance on books. However, from a discussion with the children afterwards, it was clear that they viewed books as the proper source of knowledge. Despite the fact that Sara had visited a bird park specializing in birds of prey, and although she used this in her discussions about eagles, she did not consider her knowledge from this source as something to be included in her written presentation. Also, Angela owned a dog, yet this was not seen by her as a proper focus for study and source of information: she chose 'horses' instead.

Certainly, the children learnt to value books, but it also appeared that they assumed a hidden value: namely, that books were the only valid resource to use. The corollary is that other sources of information, such as their own personal experiences, are of little or no value. In an environment which contains a wide variety of rich resources, it is unfortunate if many of them are neglected. This might include the use of oral history from members of the local community, as well as oral evidence from local 'experts' and enthusiasts which is of very real value. There are also the visual sources, such as video tape, photographs, slides, posters, computer programmes, and additional printed matter such as magazines, advertisements, newspapers, original documents and maps. Further, there is a range of artifacts which can be brought into the classroom, as well as the many forms of empirical evidence which the children can generate from their own close observations of phenomena, together with the items that they can collect and show.

The reliance on books is clearly limiting the children's learning, not only because a narrow range of skills are used but also because the transferability of skills is not enhanced. Equally, there is the danger that if books are held in such high regard it may well be that they are used uncritically because of the esteem in which they are held. Neither the

capability to compare resources, nor the understanding of their compli-
mentary use will be fostered. The opportunities for such development is
frequently available in topic work but often overlooked.

Such matters as these must be of concern to the teacher, not simply
because the child is provided with a narrow resource base but also
because the opportunity to develop a critical evaluation of available
sources is being missed. In undertaking a topic, then, it is important to
bear in mind a number of questions regarding the use of resources:

★ does the topic selected (by the teacher or the child) encourage or
require the use of more than a 'limited range of resources;

★ does the range of resources relate to children's experience and
needs in aural/oral, visual/graphic, verbal/numerical/musical
development;

★ does the variety of resources introduced to children extend their
experience of equipment, for example, video machines and
cameras, audio cassettes and recording, slide viewer/projector,
computer or camera, microscope etc;

★ what resources are available in the school, or can be obtained from
local services and the community;

★ are children encouraged to work from more than one type of
resource, and are they encouraged to compare and contrast the
information which they obtain from different resources and that
which comes from their own experience;

★ do children know how to record and present their findings
through a variety of media, for example, writing, drawing,
modelling, drama, posters, tapes, photographs etc;

★ how are children helped to approach sources critically, to recognize their limitations or partiality regarding the content and/or the
medium? are they also encouraged to be critical of their work in
the same way?

Stereotyping: Gender and Race in Resources

Cameo 3

The focus of the topic for half a term is to be 'the world of
work'. The 8 and 9-year-olds are examining the jobs people do

by drawing on information from their own families and their school environment. They are moving on to widen their understanding of work, through studies based on a range of secondary sources including books, television programmes and topic packs, which relate to jobs in the UK and abroad. The pictures and text present a wide range of (mostly white male) workers, though some women are shown in the caring jobs or in clothing manufacture. Some blacks are included — most often in unskilled jobs. The children are also considering the jobs they might like to do and those they would not like to do.

Many assumptions and values were embedded within the resources supplied in this learning situation. In particular, certain dimensions from the 'world of work' were missing, for example, work done in the home and that which is not paid. Also, there was no reference to lack of work and those not in work. Further, there was no attempt to challenge the assumption that the 'world of work' was predominantly a white male world, particularly the prestigious aspects of that world.

These are issues which have received a great deal of attention in terms of educational rhetoric in recent years. Clearly, it is difficult for schools to update their library collections frequently, and it also takes time for publishers to respond to new requests. Such materials, therefore, make certain demands of teachers. In particular, it could mean that teachers might need to take positive steps to intervene in the children's learning in order to make sure that they do not use such secondary sources in an uncritical fashion. Children need to be encouraged to consider the value and nature of different kinds of work as well as how much and in what ways the workers are valued. The discussions arising from such a topic would need to help to deepen children's understanding of a broad definition of the 'world of work' and of the origins, purposes and consequences of existing stereotypes.

One of the potential dangers of topic work is that it can lend itself to the uncritical development or reinforcement of stereotypes. This may come about through general coverage of a theme, too narrow a focus on specific, innocuous topics or in the failure to be prepared to look at it in a variety of contexts. Yet the opportunity topic offers to challenge the growth of uncritical assumptions and values in resources is considerable.

In order to achieve this the following questions could serve as a guideline:

* in identifying a theme for topic work, how shall I define that theme, and what assumptions am I making in doing so;
* in what areas does this topic offer opportunities for children to broaden and deepen their understanding, and in what ways might this challenge their existing attitudes or knowledge;
* what questions do I need to ask the children in order to help them to recognize and analyze their views;
* how should I help the children to reflect upon the resources in order to help them recognize and analyze the implicit values? (see checklists 1 and 2 at the end of this chapter).

Controversial Issues

Cameo 4

The theme for the class of top infants is one in the school's environmental studies scheme: the teachers had chosen litter in the school buildings and grounds as the starting point.

The work is developing a number of strands through such questions as 'what is litter', 'where is it found', 'what materials does it consist of', 'how did it get there', 'what can be done to get rid of it'.

The children are mapping litter sightings, collecting/ sorting/graphically recording litter, and are doing experiments as to its composition, change/decay and how best to dispose of it. This is being tackled at the school level with regard to the best siting of bins, and at the local level by contacting the local council refuse depot.

The children are very motivated and the discussions have heightened their concern and knowledge about the wider issues of pollution in their neighbourhood. Their sense of responsibility is increasing as is their desire to take positive action. However, the children's action is being restricted to within the school boundaries as the teacher feels that children should not become involved in issues which could arouse local passions.

This kind of experience highlights another dimension of the hidden values which may exist in topic work. Many topics have the potential to encourage children to consider their personal and collective responsibility towards issues which might be raised through examining the area of study. A logical next step could be to take action. A teacher has to decide whether to avoid controversial issues and stick to bland, descriptive, safe topics, or, if willing to address controversial issues, how far to go in pursuing them.

Depending on where a teacher might stand on this question, the messages that children could take away will vary in the different kinds of topic work they might experience. It may be that children will come to believe that what is studied in school can only raise questions rather than provide answers, as these come from higher 'authorities' which cannot themselves be questioned. Or, that having identified questions and raised expectations, children are then left with a sense of frustration, failure and powerlessness if their desire for action is suspended before they have tested and discovered the limits for themselves.

Another message could be that enquiry, analysis and investigation involves a recognition that there is more than one viewpoint, that individuals have to make their own personal decisions on issues, that some concerns are unresolvable. Or, a further message might be that school has little to do with reality as it is in the outside world (or even in the school grounds).

The problem for the teacher, of whether to tackle controversial issues or to avoid them, is a crucial one. For instance, at a policy level, the teacher has to consider what will count as acceptable study by an increasing number of parties: colleagues, headteacher, parents, governors. Hence, topics which might challenge the credibility of traditional 'English history', or which encourage children to reflect on the experience of racism, the proposed change in the layout of the roads near the school, the availability of facilities for the disabled in the local shopping centre, or on issues about graffiti, ill-lit underpasses and litter around the school could each meet with opposition from those 'responsible' for the school curriculum, because of a clash of values.

A further reason, at a pedagogical level, for concern about handling controversial issues is the fact that teachers may be uncertain as to how to approach such topics. Good advice has been limited, and what exists tends to be aimed at secondary teachers, although some is of help to primary teachers (Fisher and Hicks, 1985; Pettman, 1984).

Another psychological reason for avoiding controversial issues is the view that primary children are 'too young' to understand, that they cannot appreciate another person's point of view, and that they cannot make such decisions. However, evidence is growing that children can in fact do all of these things (Pollard, 1987; Bruner and Haste, 1987), given a supportive context and an issue relevant to them.

Hence, topic work which explores social, moral, political and economic concerns should not be avoided. But, in tackling such controversial issues a number of important questions need to be born in mind:

* do I believe that education is about enabling children to become well-informed and well-skilled, and do I also believe that children should learn to make and to justify decisions and value judgments;
* do I recognize that controversy is part of life outside (and inside) the classroom and that learning to respond thoughtfully is an important part of growing up;
* do I recognize that children, on entry to school, have values and opinions of their own, and am I aware of these in their interaction with me and with others;
* do I believe that it is part of the teacher's job to help children explore their own and others' beliefs;
* how do I ensure and provide opportunities for children to examine themes with a range of viewpoints, and do I deliberately introduce topics which will draw out divergent opinions;
* when controversial issues arise, do I
  — ensure access to a range of evidence and views;
  — encourage children to be open about their own views, while respecting privacy;
  — challenge bias and prejudice as it arises;
  — remain alert to my own bias and prejudice;
  — foster qualities of sensitivity, empathy, fairness, respect, readiness to listen, rationality and imagination;
  — encourage children to examine information critically, to recognize rhetoric, to question assumptions and to explore their own responses;
  — do I inform the head, parents and others about the topic we are doing, and do I base our examination of controversial issues on an explicit set of principles (see checklist 3, drawn from Bridges, 1986).

Conclusions

The premise of this chapter was that values are transmitted to children through the topic work they are doing. This is not just in terms of the values explicitly explored, but also through the implicit and unrecognized values that are part of the children's 'received curriculum'. Such a view holds that whatever the children do, how they are taught, what the expectations and standards expected are, and what they are taught are all dependent on the values held by the teacher. Thus, teaching, learning and the curriculum are not value-free.

Hence, topic work — in what it includes and excludes, in who decides that, in how it is developed, in the amount of time set aside for it — is value-laden. The foregoing 'cameos', which focused on organization/grouping, types/quality of resources and on content, have highlighted some of these hidden aspects. The purpose has been to encourage its recognition and thence its examination. We might begin by examining the values inherent in our own practice.

Checklist 1: Considering Existing Stereotyping in Resources

Question the usefulness of resources which:

* ★ simplify information to the point of distortion, partiality, bias;
* ★ simplify differences in jobs, life styles, conditions, cultures etc. to the level of sweeping generalization;
* ★ present tasks, roles, people, cultures in cliches, caricatures, fantastical or mythical forms without alternative evidence;
* ★ attribute differential value to particular jobs, roles, customs;
* ★ are out-of-date;
* ★ give ready-made conclusions;
* ★ portray living beings as unable to influence events;
* ★ imply that things happen, or that people take actions, which can be taken for granted and need no explanation;
* ★ convey a perspective from one cultural/social standpoint, assuming that a single set of norms is universally accepted;
* ★ portray activities/people/roles/cultures in a condescending, patronizing or derogatory way.

Checklist 2: **Evaluating Sexism and Racism in Resources**

Many checklists are available (for example, Clark, 1979; Preiswick, 1980; Fisher and Hicks, 1985; Klein, 1985). The following questions identify a number of common concerns.

Illustrations

★ is the proportion of females to males equally balanced;
★ are females and males shown in both modern and traditional roles and contexts;
★ are a range of cultural groups presented in a positive way;
★ are ethnic people shown in modern and traditional roles and contexts;
★ are a range of female/male/ethnic models presented in decisive and active roles, with whom children can identify;
★ are people shown as individuals, not as group representatives;
★ are illustrations up-to-date and free from propaganda;
★ do the illustrations extend the text and enable children to use evidence in them to answer questions and to raise further issues?

Language

★ is the language a-sexual in that male and female pronouns are used appropriately;
★ are terms such as people, community, society used to include both genders, and all ethnic and social groupings without differentiation;
★ are there examples of 'loaded' or inappropriate words, for example, native, primitive, manmade, policeman;
★ where speech is used, is the language or dialect of the people talking used with respect;
★ are culture-specific and specialist terms used in context, and clearly explained?;
★ is the text written in such a way as to eliminate damaging feelings based on stereotypes.

Content

★ does the text present a balanced view of male/female images;

★ does the text avoid implying that male/female roles are universal and unchangeable, or that either is superior;

★ does the text portray a range of cultures accurately and appropriately;

★ does the text refer to all human conditions, including those which are not beautiful or popular;

★ does the text offer a range of perspectives, not assuming that any one individual, country, race or religion is superior;

★ does the text give attention to everyday tasks and activities and not just the exotic;

★ does the text present factual information accurately, is it broadly-based, identifying the contributions to human achievements from all societies around the world, both past and present?

Checklist 3: Principles Underlying the Introduction of Controversial Issues into Topic Work (after Bridges, 1986).

* respect for persons, including the child's, the parent's and the teacher's right to hold opinions which differ, and a willingness to understand those views;

* concern to foster and extend the personal autonomy of children as reflective thinkers, including cultivating understanding and self-confidence which are conditions both of free-choice and the capacity of decision-making;

* honest acknowledgement of the true nature and status of opinions, which includes unequivocal recognition of the uncertainty, partiality and controversial nature of judgment, as well as recognition of the problematic distinction between fact and value;

* readiness on the part of the teacher to detach own opinions from the authority derived from the professional role, so that they rest on the authority of reason alone;

* concern that pupils grasp the reasons, evidence and argument that underpin any opinions offered;

* concern to teach the nature of and basis for the controversial issue, and not just the conclusion from any one perspective;

* concern to cultivate a constant alertness to and critical analysis of beliefs, values and opinions which might otherwise be taken for granted, especially one's own.

Appendix: Planning and Topic

The move towards articulating detailed curriculum policy in all curriculum areas increases the need to analyze and record our teaching plans as well as the children's progress.

There are three main aspects of this:

(i)   curriculum forecasts;
(ii) lesson/session plans and evaluations;
(iii) record-keeping.

1 Curriculum Forecasts

In order to begin to prepare for a new topic it is important to gather some background information about:

(i)   the individual children;
(ii) their previous experience of topic work;
(iii) the school; its policies, its resources, the community and the locality.

This is particularly pertinent for a student teacher or new teacher coming into the school for the first time.

Preparation and Observations

Teachers need to collect information about the children — through observation, discussion, analysis — and also to record all such findings, so that specific needs can be identified. Against this background a general curriculum forecast and a particular learning session can be planned.

The following general aspects will have to be decided:

(i)   What are the present capabilities of the children?

(ii)   What topic work have they experienced in the past?

(iii)   Is there a policy or guidelines for topic work?

(iv)   Are there any excursions/events already planned on a school basis that could be a stimulus, or distraction ...?

(v)   Are there any constraints imposed by simultaneous demands from other teachers or event happening in the school (for example, play rehearsals, school photo, sports practices) which could effect your planning of such activities?

Initial Planning

More precise details can now be considered;
For example, what specific objectives are appropriate — in terms of skills, attitudes, concepts and knowledge in intellectual, social, physical/practical, moral and aesthetic domains?

The following steps can be taken WITH the children, or outlined before if preferred:

(i)   choose a topic for investigation ...
        for example, a problem to solve, an issue to consider;
        a concept to explore, an interest to extend.

(ii)   list questions that it raises and to which you and the children want to find the answers ...

(iii)   sort out what you have got so far and think what the children might learn from searching for these answers:
        (a)   think in terms of component skills, attitudes, concepts and knowledge ...
        (b)   and in terms of aspects such as contexts, locations, learning procedures and resources ...

(iv)   identify the audience with whom you will share your findings and to whom you will present them ...

(v)   decide to what extent, at each of these stages, you will encourage the children to make the decisions and plan the topic. What will they learn from doing this?

Lastly, it is important to consider:

(i)   What organizational demands will these plans make in terms of children, adults, time, space, environment, resources?

(ii)   How will the progress of the session and the progress of the children be monitored?

Recording Curriculum Plans: Grid/flow Chart/web

See chapters 2 and 9.

CURRICULUM FORECASTS, AN EXAMPLE

Choose a topic, like the problem of Road Safety ... (with 9–11-year-olds).

Second, the questions:

(i)   has anyone ever had an accident, what kinds of accidents happen most often, what is it like inside an ambulance;

(ii)   how quickly can you stop on your bike, how can you make a bike safer,

(iii)   which is the 'safest' colour for cars;

(iv)   how can blind people cross roads, how do you train their dogs, do they have to pay for them?

Third, consider the following aspects:

(i)   identify the social contexts: working alone, in a group, as a class,

(ii)   identify the physical locations: classroom, library, school grounds, trip out,

(iii)   identify the learning procedures:

    (a)   observing and monitoring traffic;

    (b)   listening/talking to the ambulance crew;

    (c)   reading about guidedogs, writing letters to 'experts';

    (d)   designing a questionnaire (to find out who has and who has not had an accident);

    (e)   doing a survey of the local roads to identify hazards for blind and disabled people;

    (f)   planning a 'fair test' to find out about breaking distances of own bicycles ...

(iv)   identify resources:

    (a)   for information ... telephone, books, accident statistics;

    (b)   for exploration ... observation schedule, stop-watch, map;

    (c)   for presentation ... paper, glue, material etc, for pictures/models/folders.

Fourth, which audience:

    (i)   the teacher as assessor, the school during assembly;

    (ii)   the class, everyone for an 'open evening' ...

Fifth, collaboration throughout the topic:

    (i)   how will the children participate in the planning;

    (ii)   providing and implementation of the topic; and

    (iii)   most importantly, the constant reviewing and evaluating,

The children will need to negotiate amongst themselves about what to do,

    who will do it,

    how to do it,

and how well it has been done.

    When analyzing the learning in terms of skills, attitudes, concepts, and knowledge, you could use the following checklist as an initial framework:

    (i)   skills: personal/social (turn-taking, sharing, supporting); physical/practical (moving, balancing, using equipment); intellectual (observing, questioning, hypothesizing, reasoning, testing, evaluating, imagining, inventing); communicating (oracy, literacy, numeracy, graphicacy);

    (ii)   attitudes: curiosity, perserverance, initiative, confidence, open-mindedness, trust, honesty, responsibility, respect;

    (iii)   concepts: continuity/change, cause/effect, authenticity, sequence/duration, nature/purpose, power, energy, interdependence/adaptation, interaction

> ... also, in relation to road safety, distance, speed,
> direction, conspicuity, visibility, road users, road
> usage, roadway 'furniture' ...

Having analyzed the topic this way — across-the-curriculum — check
the following:

(i)   is there a balance between the range of skills, attitudes,
       concepts and knowledge;
(ii)   is there an appropriate progression between activities which
       offer incremental/extension/enrichment/reinforcement of the
       intended learning?;
(iii) is there sufficient differentiation in the levels demanded to suit
       the whole ability spread within the class?;
(iv)   is there evidence of continuity and cohesion between the
       different activities?;
(v)   is there clear coherence between the intended learning goals and
       the organizational support for the learning/teaching processes?

This method of planning curriculum activities and managing the
learning/teaching sessions should help to:

(i)   encourage and extend children's learning;
(ii)   diagnose difficulties and opportunities for development;
(iii) motivate, maintain and monitor the learning experiences.

'Lesson' Plan for Teaching/learning Session

These plans should enable you (or any other reader) to visualize the
session. In a session where groups or individuals are working on
different tasks, it is important to make clear who is doing what. If tasks
are 'continuing' or on a 'rotational' basis, it is sufficient for the plan to just
mention 'see above'.

Plans should make clear the following aspects:

WHAT is going to happen:
— the FOCUS of the session.
    This may be in terms of knowledge content,
    for example, safety features of a bicycle, the effect of colour (of cars
    or coats) in relation to their 'conspicuity'.

WHY this choice has been made:
— with reference to the OBJECTIVES in terms of skills, attitudes, knowledge and concepts.

HOW these intentions will be implemented:
— identifying the main teaching STRATEGIES in relation to motivation, management, monitoring,
for example, questioning, demonstrations, discussions, instruction, negotiation ...

WHEN these different strategies will be used
— estimating the TIMING and TRANSITION of activities in particular how the session will begin;
be sustained;
will end.

WITH WHOM the different strategies and activities will be used
— organization and GROUPING arrangements.
WITH WHAT the children will work.
— anticipating and, where necessary, preparing the required RESOURCES

and, of course,
the plan has to be able to be flexible and respond to the children, on that day, at that time; the participants have to be able to expect the unexpected ...
Review questions to check that your plan is comprehensive enough:

1   How are you going to introduce the session?
2   What links are there with previous work and with the children's experiences?
3   What role will the children play in planning the activities?
4   Are you and the children sure of the 'ground rules' in terms or expectations and standards of work?
5   Are the routine procedures for avoiding bottle-necks well known i.e. when children want help (support, particular spellings, pencils sharpened), what to do when a task is completed?
6   How much flexibility will there be in this session for the children to initiate new avenues of work?
7   In terms of work to be finished, how long do you estimate each task will take?

8 Have you planned for every child to experience changes of pace during the course of a session (for example, some listening, discussion, practical work, reading, recording, reflecting ...)?
9 Which of the tasks are intended to reinforce/extend?
10 How will you use adult helpers in the classroom?
11 Have you planned how you will manage the variety of tasks and the different demands they will make at different times during the session?
12 How will the children disperse to their various tasks?
13 How will the resources be made available?

LESSON PLAN: AN EXAMPLE (Focus and objectives)
Week One — What Will They Learn?
Age of children: 6–7 years
Focus: Concepts of danger and safety in relation to roads and cars
Activity: watch SuperTed video (10 min) and discuss,
  examine colleague's bicycle and identify safety features
  draw and label diagram of bicycle with safety features (to be used for 'Beetle' type game)
  construct a 'dice' for use in the game.

Skills	Attitudes	Concepts	Knowledge
		Road safety in general	
	Awareness of danger [SuperTed video]		
Turn-taking in discussion			
			How to cross the road (Green X Code)
Identify safety features Check brakes lights etc. Drawing from observation	Responsibility for prevention	Cause/effect of accidents	Parts of a bicycle
Labelling diagram	Neatness and pride in presentation	Representation of information	Parts of a bicycle
Information skills (using spelling book)			
Constructing a dice	Importance of exactness	Probability	

14   Have you allowed time for yourself to monitor, encourage, engage in extended learning conferences?

15   Have you considered how you will draw the session to a close, for example, getting feedback from the children, encouraging the children to support each other and to evaluate their own work, emphasizing the learning points and their applicability?

16   Have you allowed time for packing away?

17   Have you got a store of ideas for 2/5/10 minute activities in case you finish early?

18   How will you evaluate the session, what criteria will you use, and what kind of evidence will you need to look for?

Evaluation of the Learning Session

It is vitally important to monitor the learning sessions and to note down moments of progress or puzzlement, items to reinforce or extend for individuals and groups.

There are many different ways of noting such information. Initially it is often useful to use a 'diary' format which, although rather discursive, is full and detailed. This anecdotal form needs then to be reflected upon so that significant details can be extracted. The following framework of questions could be used:

(i)   What have the children learnt?
(ii)   Was it worthwhile?
(iii)   What have I learnt?
(iv)   How can I use this information for future planning?

Later, a more analytic approach can be adopted, and significant information selected for immediate recording. This could be coded straight onto checklists or appraisal sheets, though these usually are improved by also having an open-ended comments section where elaborations can be noted.

The checklist criteria should be the same as the objectives. Different levels of achievement can be indicated by a range of 'cross-hatching', for example

□	◁	⊠	■
no understanding	some understanding	secure understanding	able to apply and extend

Bibliography

ALEXANDER, R.J. (1984) *Primary Teaching*, London, Holt, Rinehart and Winston.

AVANN, P. (1983) 'Information skills in primary schools: An investigation', MEd thesis, University of Loughborough.

AVANN, P. (Ed) (1985) *Teaching Information Skills in the Primary School*, London, Edward Arnold.

BARROW, R. (1981) *The Philosophy of Schooling*, Brighton, Wheatsheaf.

BARNES, D. (1975) *From Communication to Curriculum*, Harmondsworth, Penguin.

BARNES, D. (1978) *Language in the Classroom*, Milton Keynes, Open University.

BASSEY, M. (1978) *Nine Hundred Primary School Teachers*, Slough, NFER.

BLYTH, A. *et al* (1976) *Place, Time and Society 8–13; Curriculum Planning in History, Geography and Social Science*, London, Collins.

BOARD OF EDUCATION (1931) *The Primary School* (The Hadow Report) London, HMSO.

BONNETT, M. (1986) 'Child-centredness and the problems of structure in project work', *Cambridge Journal of Education*, 16, 1.

BRADLEY, H. *et al* (1985) *Developing Pupils' Thinking Through Topic Work*, London, Longmans/SCDC.

BRANSFORD, J.D. *et al* (1984) 'Cognition and adaptation: The importance of learning to learn' in HARVEY, J. (Ed.) *Cognition, Social Behaviour and the Environment*, Englewood Cliffs, Erlbaum.

BRIDGES, D. (1986) 'Dealing with controversy in the school curriculum' in WELLINGTON, J. (Ed.) *Controversial Issues in the Curriculum*, Oxford, Blackwells.

BRUNER, J.S. (1966) *Toward a Theory of Instruction*, London, Belknap Press of Harvard University.

BRUNER, J.S. (1977) *The Process of Education*, Cambridge, MA, Harvard University Press.

BRUNER, J. and HASTE, H. (1987) *Making Sense*, London, Methuen.

CATCHPOLE, G. (1986) *Your Topic Work in School*, London, New Education Press.

CENTRAL ADVISORY COUNCIL ON EDUCATION (1967) *Children and Their Primary Schools* (The Plowden Report), London, HMSO.

CHAPMAN, J. (1983) *Developing Reading*, London, Heinemann.

CHAPMAN, L.J. (1987) *Reading from 5–11*, Milton Keynes, Open University Press.

CLARK, B. (Ed.) (1979) *The Changing World and the Primary School*, London, Centre for World Development Education.

CLIFT, P. *et al* (1981) *Record Keeping in Primary Schools*, (Schools Council Research Studies) London, Macmillan.

COX, C.B. and DYSON, A.E. (1969) *Fight For Education: A Black Paper*, London, Critical Quarterly Society.

DEARDEN, R. (1976) *Problems in Primary Education*, London, Routledge and Kegan Paul.

DEPARTMENT OF EDUCATION AND SCIENCE. (1975) *A Language for Life* (The Bullock Report), London, HMSO. (1978) *Primary Education in England: Survey by HM Inspectors of Schools*, London, HMSO. (1979) *Aspects of Secondary Education: Survey by HMI*, London, HMSO. (1982) *Education 5–9: An Illustrative Survey of Eighty First Schools in England*, London, HMSO. (1985a) *Education 8–12 in Combined and Middle Schools: An HMI Survey*, London, HMSO. (1985b) *The Curriculum from 5–16: Curriculum Matters no. 2*, HMI discussion document, London, HMSO. (1987) *The National Curriculum 5–16: Consultative Document*, London, HMSO.

DONALDSON, M. (1978) *Children's Minds*, London, Fontana.

EASEN, P. (1985) *Making School Centred INSET Work*, London, Croom Helm.

EYSENK, H. J. and COOKSON, D. (1969) 'Personality in primary school children, 1: Ability and Achievement,' *British Journal of Educational Psychology*, 39, 109–122.

FISHER, S. and HICKS, D. (1985) *World Studies 8–13: A Teacher's Handbook*, Edinburgh, Oliver and Boyd.

GAGNÉ, R. (1975) *Essentials of Learning Instruction*, New York, Holt, Rinehart and Winston.

GEORGE, F. (1978) Guidelines for the development and evaluation of unbiased educational materials, in SPRING, B. (Ed.) *Perspectives in Non-Sexist Early Education*, New York, Teachers College Press.

GRAY, H. (1982) 'Organization development in the primary school' in RICHARDS, C. (Ed.) *New Directions in Primary Education*, Lewes, Falmer Press.

GUNNING, S., GUNNING, D. and WILSON, J. (1981) *Topic Teaching in the Primary School*, London, Arnold.

HAMAIDE, A. (1925) *The Delcroy Class*, London, Dent.

HARRI-AUGSTEIN, S. *et al*(1982) *Reading to Learn*, London, Methuen.

KAGAN, J. *et al*, (1964) 'Reflection-impulsivity and reading ability in primary grade children' *Child Development* 36, 609–628.

KAGAN, J. and KOGAN, N. (1970) 'Individual variation in cognitive processes, in Mussel, P. (Ed.) *Carmichael's Manual of Child Psychology*, 3rd. ed. vol.1 New York, Wiley.

KLEIN, G. (1985) *Reading into Racism*, London, Routledge and Kegan Paul

LANE, R. (1981) *Project Work in the Primary School*, Preston Curriculum Development Centre.

LAWSON, K. (1979) 'The politics of primary curricula', *Education 3–13*, 7, 1, pp. 23–6.

LEITH, S. (1981) 'Project work: An enigma' in SIMON, B. and WILLCOCKS, J. (Eds.) *Research and Practice in the Primary School*, London, Routledge and Kegan Paul.

LUNZER, E. and GARDNER, K. (1979) *The Effective Use of Reading*, London, Heinemann for the Schools Council.

MARLAND, M. (Ed.) (1981) *Information Skills in the Secondary School*, Schools Council Curriculum Bulletin 9, London, Methuen.

MEYER, J.F. (1984) 'Organizational Aspects of Text: Effects on Reading Comprehension and Application: for the classroom', in FLOOD, J. (Ed.) *Promoting Reading Comprehension* I.R.A. Newark, Delaware.

NEVILLE, M. (1977) 'The development of the ability to use a book' *Reading*, 11, 3, pp. 18–21.

NEVILLE, M. and PUGH A. (1975) 'Reading ability and ability to use a book — A study of middle school children', *Reading*, 9, 3, pp. 23–31.

NEVILLE, M. and PUGH, A. (1977) 'Ability to use a book: The effect of teaching', *Reading*, 11, 3, pp. 13–18.

NISBET, J. and SHUKSMITH, J. (1986) *Learning Strategies*, London, Routledge and Kegan Paul.

PASK, G. (1976) 'Styles and strategies of learning', *British Journal of Educational Psychology*, 46, 128–148.

PERERA, K. (1984) *Children's Writing and Reading*, Oxford, Blackwells.

PETTMAN, R. (1984) *Teaching for Human Rights*, Richmond, Victoria, Australia, Hodja Educational Resources Cooperative.

POLLARD, A. (Ed.) (1987) *Children and Their Primary Schools*, Lewes, Falmer Press.

PREISWICK, R. (Ed.) (1980) *The Slant of the Pen*, London, World Council of Churches.

RICHARDS, C. (1982) 'Curriculum consistency' in RICHARDS, C. (Ed.) *New Directions in Primary Education*, Lewes, Falmer Press.

SAYER, B. (1979) 'An investigation into the acquisition of study skills by children aged 11–13', MEd, Edge Hill College/University of Lancaster.

SCHOOLS COUNCIL (1972) *Science 5–13*, London, Methuen.

SCHOOLS COUNCIL (1983) *Primary Practice, Working Paper 75*, London, Methuen.

SCHOOLS CURRICULUM DEVELOPMENT COMMITTEE (1985) *Topic Work Resource Bank*, London, SCDC.

SELMES, I. (1986) *Improving Study Skills*, London, Hodder and Stoughton.

SHELDON, S. (1986) 'Representing comprehension' in ROOT, B. (Ed.) *Resources for Reading*, Basingstoke, Macmillan (for UKRA).

SOUTHGATE, V. et al (1981) *Extending Beginning Reading*, London, Heinemann for Schools Council.

STEWART, N. (1987) 'A triumph of organization', *Times Educational Supplement*, 3 April, p. 22.

STONIER, T. (1982) 'Changes in Western society' in RICHARDS, C. (Ed.) *New Directions in Primary Education*, Lewes, Falmer Press.

TANN, C.S. (1981) 'Grouping and group work' in SIMON, B. and WILLCOCKS, J. (Eds) *Research and Practice in the Primary Classroom*, London, Routledge and Kegan Paul.

TANN, C.S. (1987) 'Topic work: A mismatch of perceptions', *Reading*, 21, 1.

THOMAS, N. (1982) 'Topics in turmoil', *Times Educational Supplement*, 1 October.

TORRANCE, E.P. (1962) *Guiding Creative Talent*, Englewood Cliffs, New Jersey, Prentice Hall.

WINKWORTH, E. (1977) *User Education in Schools*, London, British Library Research and Development Department.

WITKIN, H.A. (1977) 'Field-dependent cognitive styles and their educational implications', *Review of Educational Research*, 1, 1–64.

WRAY, D. (1985) *Teaching Information Skills though Project Work*, London, Hodder and Stoughton.

Notes on Contributors

Margaret Armitage has taught 5–8 year olds for eighteen years and is now deputy head of an Oxfordshire school. She has a particular interest in reading, oral and writing development. An INSET secondment and involvement in a working party on topic work caused a reappraisal of her approach to this in her classroom.

John Barrett has taught for twenty years in primary schools in rural, urban and development areas. He has been a Head and is now a Primary Adviser in West Sussex. His interests are in 'language and learning' and in developing a curriculum that can accommodate children's own perspectives of their world.

Simon Catling taught in ILEA primary schools for twelve years before moving to Oxford Polytechnic. He is Chair of the Education Committee of the Geographical Association and has published many articles and classroom books relating to geography and environmental studies.

Elaine Gethins entered the teaching profession as a mature student. She has now taught for nine years, throughout the primary age range. Her membership of the local Writer's Workshop helps her in finding ways to support the children in their topic work writing, particularly in their awareness of audience.

Robert Hayes has taught for many years in Buckinghamshire and is currently Deputy Head of a first school. He has undertaken further studies at Wall Hall and Buckinghamshire Colleges of Higher Education as well as at Bulmershe, where he completed a MEd thesis which is the basis for his contribution in this book.

Joe Johnson	has taught for fifteen years and has been head of an Oxfordshire school for the last eight years. He has been closely involved in developing computer-based education in the county and was seconded to the Micro Technology Advisory Service for a year.
Stephen Long	has taught for eleven years in Buckinghamshire middle schools. During a year long secondment to Oxford Polytechnic he studied topic work in a number of local schools. Having had responsibility for most areas of the curriculum, he now holds responsibility for Topic Work and School Liaison.
Tina Ruff	has taught for ten years in Cheshire primary schools and for ten years in Oxfordshire. An OU course in maths across the curriculum stimulated her appreciation of 'real' learning experiences and of the unity of learning.
Sarah Tann	has experienced a wide range of classrooms, as both teacher (from pre-school to higher education) and as researcher (on the ORACLE project). For the last three years she has been working closely with teachers, children and students to learn more about topic work and to find ways of developing it. She has worked at Oxford Polytechnic since 1982 and her responsibilities include leadership of the language courses for BEd students, supervision of student school experience and module leadership on the MEd programme.

Index